THEY CAME FROM AWAY

YANKS, BRITS AND CAPE BRETON

David and Pamela Newton

iUniverse, Inc.
New York   Bloomington

David and Pam Newton

THEY CAME FROM AWAY
YANKS, BRITS AND CAPE BRETON

Copyright © 2010 by David and Pamela Newton

All rights reserved. No part of this book may be used or reproduced by any means, graphic, electronic, or mechanical, including photocopying, recording, taping or by any information storage retrieval system without the written permission of the publisher except in the case of brief quotations embodied in critical articles and reviews.

iUniverse books may be ordered through booksellers or by contacting:
iUniverse
1663 Liberty Drive
Bloomington, IN 47403
www.iuniverse.com
1-800-Authors (1-800-288-4677)

Because of the dynamic nature of the Internet, any Web addresses or links contained in this book may have changed since publication and may no longer be valid. The views expressed in this work are solely those of the author and do not necessarily reflect the views of the publisher, and the publisher hereby disclaims any responsibility for them.

ISBN: 978-1-4502-2416-1 (pbk)
ISBN: 978-1-4502-2417-8 (ebk)

Printed in the United States of America
iUniverse rev. date: 4/27/10

"History is the essence of innumerable biographies."

Thomas Carlyle. 1838.

For Elizabeth, Michael, Christopher, Sandra, Laura Jane and Andrew.

TABLE OF CONTENTS

INTRODUCTION	1
PREFACE — THE FIRST BRITS AND YANKS	5
PRINCE HENRY SINCLAIR	8
LORD OCHILTREE, THE FIRST CAPE BRETONER	14
"LORD JEFFREY AMHERST WAS A SOLDIER OF THE KING."	19
ENSIGN PRENTIES – SURVIVOR	29
LAW AND ORDER – EARLY CAPE BRETON	33
WYNYARD AND THE 33rd	37
DAVID TAITT - SURVEYOR AND INDIAN AGENT	42
THE CANTANKEROUS MAYOR	53
BALL BROTHERS - PARADOXES IN AN AGE OF PARADOX	63
CAPTAIN THOMAS CRAWLEY	73
JOHN AND MARY LEITCH – PRESS-GANGED AND SHIP-WRECKED	77
THANKFULL AND MARY – THE COSSITS AND McLEODS	82
MURDER AND THE WASHED UP SAILORS	94
RICHARD BROWN - WHEN COAL BECAME KING	99
THE LONELY LOVER – A TRAVELER'S TALE	109

WILLIAM PENN HUSSEY - HUCKSTER	114
PHILIP WORGAN	118
HENRY MELVILLE WHITNEY - "FINDER OF SYDNEY"	125
ARTHUR J. MOXHAM – BUILDER OF STEEL PLANTS AND STONE CASTLES	129
ONE OF MANY	137
BLACK STEELWORKERS FROM ALABAMA	141
CAPTAIN HORSFALL AND THE SCHOOL FOR SCANDAL	144
ROBERT J. PEARY - NORTHWARD HO!	150
"THOSE DARING MEN AND THEIR FLYING MACHINES"	158
JACK HOLMES - HANGMAN	164
"GUS' EDWARDS – COAL MINER TO AIR MARSHAL	172
COLONIAL LOGS SET SAIL	181
BERYL MARKHAM – "STRAIGHT ON TILL MORNING"	185
THREE WRITERS	193
TOM KENT - OK, SIGNED TK	201
EPILOGUE	209
NOTES	211

INTRODUCTION

New York City in mid-August can be almost unbearable. As I headed in from Long Island, trapped for too long in the humidity of the subway, I wondered just why I was there. Pam, showing remarkable good sense, stayed at home in our midget apartment with the fan blowing full blast, while I headed for an office near 42nd Street. By the time my train reached mid-town Fifth Avenue I had had enough. I would walk down Fifth to the office.

Coming out of the subway I was faced by an incredible sight. There, in the window of the Canadian Consulate General's Office, was an enormous photograph of an iceberg. And in the bottom left hand corner an Eskimo kayaked happily away. This, I sensed immediately, was the place for me. I was directed upstairs one floor to the immigration department. I had no idea what Pam or I would do in Canada, if we could get there, nor even what area should be our destination, but a woman in the line ahead of me gave me the clue. The immigration officer asked her what she wanted to do "Farm" she replied. "Doing what?" she was asked. "Well" she said, "I want to raise baby chicks to supply laying hens to the commercial market. I thought it would be a good idea if I started with a thousand hens and a thousand cockerels." The immigration officer was surprised. "You know" he said, "You don't really need that many cockerels. A few dozen would be quite sufficient." The would-be immigrant farmer was annoyed. "You men" she snapped, "You're all the same" and walked out. There was my lead. If she could contemplate farming with that level of knowledge, why not me?

The immigration officer had clearly been put in a good mood by the encounter and faced me with a broad smile as I answered his preliminary questions. "Where do you want to go?" "I've no idea" "How much money do you have?" "None", I answered. "Then you'd better go to Cape Breton. No one there has any money either" and gave me a pamphlet called "Farms for sale in Nova Scotia".

Unfortunately that wasn't the end of it. Although we could and did buy a very small farm in the middle of Cape Breton we still had so little money that we could not be considered immigrants. But there was a loophole. We could go as "summer residents" for a strictly limited period of six months in the year. And so it was, in the spring of 1963 well before the later influx of hippies, we headed north with one baby, a dog, some furniture and several boxes of books. Later we became permanent residents and then citizens. More than forty years on we are still here.

It is a peculiarity of Cape Bretoners and possibly most islanders, that only those born and raised on the island are regarded as true natives. Others, no matter how long they may have been here, are "From Away". So the authentic islanders in their own eyes, the Scottish and Irish in particular, who have a high regard for their family origins and who cherish their roots regard those who moved to the island, no matter how long ago, as "awayers". It may be used to excuse a real or imagined deficiencies, such as "he's from away" with an implied "poor fellow". Few realize the enormous impact these "awayers" have had on island history.

This island attitude may have deep implications. For example, in more than two hundred years of permanent European settlement during most of which time the death penalty was the sentence for murder, only "awayers" were ever hanged. More of that later.

But what a collection these awayers have been, particularly those from south of the border or from Britain. They include a would-be murderer, a mayor of New York City, who achieved high office here and another, a drifter from Arizona who ended on the gallows; a Scot, who first settled in Florida, led a band of a thousand Creeks and Cherokees against American rebels and who sired a son who would become a prominent Indian leader. This list is almost endless. Hucksters and industrialists, fliers and sailors, disbanded soldiers, casual visitors. Any selection among so many must be arbitrary and so we have picked those who have appealed to our imagination. Their diversity illustrates the diversity of the island of Cape Breton that has been both pivotal and peripheral to our history.

In truth, everyone on the island – with the exception of the Mi'kmaq Indians who were settled here long before Europe even knew of North America – has his or her roots with someone from away. At first, following the expulsion of the Acadians from Nova Scotia and the French from Louisbourg and its outposts, the settlers were British, Loyalists from the American colonies and a few returning Acadians. At the beginning of the nineteenth century came the great wave of Scottish Highland immigration, so great that even today these former Scots represent the dominant culture as any glance at the local telephone directory will attest.

We, the authors, have been here for over forty years, one of us is a Yank from the United States, the other a Brit from England, so both of us are "awayers". Five of our six children are more fortunate.

By being from away we are able to pick out better than those who are not, a handful of Yanks or Brits who have made Cape Breton Island such a delightful mosaic of characters and culture. We live in a house built by the son of a Loyalist soldier from Virginia and our credentials, we believe, fit us to this task. Pamela, is directly descended from early Dutch and English settlers of New Amsterdam (now New York) and New England. David is from England and also has a slight connection "south of the border". Aside from living for six years in the United States he served for several years as an officer in the Royal Lincolnshire Regiment, the 10th Foot, whose soldiers more than two hundred years ago, were fired on by so-called patriots at Concord in the opening volley of the American War of Independence.

We arrived on Cape Breton as the snow blew across the ice on the Bras d'Or Lake. Did we choose right? Sometimes, when it seems that our farmhouse is the first landfall of blizzards leaving Greenland, we wonder. But then, when we take inventory and understand what a diversity of experience and joy has been our lot, we know just what must have been the experience of so many "from awayers". What a fortunate choice some – but not all - made. Here are a few of their stories, happy and sad. All of them but one, and that from what was a colony of Great Britain, are from places that were or became the United Kingdom or from the United States. We hope their stories help put a human face on the island history.

Preface
THE FIRST BRITS AND YANKS

Voyagers arrived on Cape Breton many years ago and there were no doubt American colonists and English among the Basques and Portuguese who scooped up the cod in the waters off the island. Yet it was the French, principally through their Fortress at Louisbourg, who made the first substantial settlement. And it was the Yanks – British though they were at the time – who first displaced them.

These American colonists fought and many died at the First Siege of Louisbourg in 1745, but when it was all over the British government in its wisdom returned it to the French in exchange for territory in India called Pondicherry. It may have been an astute political move in adding to what would soon be seen as the "Jewel in the British crown". But it failed dismally to endear those American colonists who fought in the British cause to accept the authority of London. Thirty years later the sons of those Louisbourg veterans remembered the tales learned at their father's knees and those fathers, the men who fought at Louisbourg, saw their sons march off to Bunker Hill. The men who froze at Valley Forge had been tempered by their fathers' tales of the fog and chill of Gabarus Bay. The amateur Colonial soldiers who accepted the surrender of Cornwallis at Yorktown knew they could defeat a professional army; their fathers had done the same at Louisbourg. For at Louisbourg in 1745 were sown the seeds that grew to be the United States of America.

These early American visitors who came from away had a major impact on the evolution of American history. They had an impact on Cape Breton as well for it soon became clear to London that giving Louisbourg back to the French had been a mistake and so, in the Seven Years War, in 1758, the Fortress had to be taken again – this time by troops and sailors under Jeffrey Amherst and James Wolfe. And this time it was not handed back but, stone by stone, destroyed. But the destruction does not hide the reality. The First Siege of Louisbourg by Americans from the New England colonies awoke the imaginings of what was to become the United States of America. It is not stretching the imagination too far to state that it was here in Cape Breton, at Louisbourg that the aspirations of a continent were born.

But those same aspirations tore the American colonies apart. Two territories, Nova Scotia in the north and Florida in the south, did not join the Thirteen and within the rebelling colonies there became what could be called a civil war – the first American civil war that like all civil wars tear families and communities apart.

It was a direct result of this that thousands of Loyalists, those remaining loyal to the King, poured north into Canada finally to spill over onto Cape Breton.

When land grants were proportioned out, Brits from both sides of the Atlantic arrived: disbanded soldiers like Joseph Jefferson from Virginia, and Robert Hill and Henry Lewis; displaced Loyalists like Daniel Watson, originally from Scotland but latterly of New

York, and Peter Sparling, also from New York State, whose families lost everything in the British cause; Joseph Rudderham and Charles Grant, stonemasons, who came aboard the *Blenheim* with Lt Governor DesBarres group from England. They all became neighbors and their descendants are our neighbors now.

PRINCE HENRY SINCLAIR

Just under a hundred years before Columbus discovered the New World a Scotsman, Prince Henry St. Clair of the Orkney Islands and Caithness and Baron of Rosslyn, may have discovered Nova Scotia. A growing number believe also that he landed on Cape Breton.

Those who believe that Prince Henry – more properly titled Earl St. Clair of Rosslyn – discovered Nova Scotia are convinced by an intriguing and challenging array of facts, some indisputable, others, well not quite so indisputable. The interior of Rosslyn Chapel in Scotland, built between 1446 and 1484, is famous for its many ornate carvings, particularly around its centerpiece, the "apprentice pillar", of motifs associated with the Knights Templar. One of the ornate carvings around a window in the chapel is of Indian corn, maize, which did not exist in Europe until many years later. How, many wonder, did they know of corn?

These Knights Templar, initially members of an impoverished order that vowed to protect pilgrims on there way to Jerusalem in the Middle Ages, ultimately gained great wealth, though they lost Jerusalem. So great was the indebtedness of the King of France to the

Knights that he hit upon a certain way clear his debts. He would have them all killed. The Pope, the Clement V who had moved his seat to Avignon, supported the idea, issuing the Suppression Order in 1312. The intention was elimination and although the suppression was horrifyingly successful, the results fell slightly short of the goal. Some got away. Those that did were aware that Scotland's King Robert the Bruce had refused to obey the Suppression Order because he had himself been earlier excommunicated.

A handful of these knights escaped the massacre and with what treasure they managed to retain, including say some reports the Holy Grail, made it as far as Scotland, to the Sinclair estates near Edinburgh. Their security there was far from assured. During the fourteenth century King Edward I of England, known as "the hammer of the Scots", frequently attacked Scotland. When the Scots beat the English in 1303 at the Battle of Rosslyn the king of England, this time Edward II, decided to take another crack at his northern neighbours. Yet another failure, this time at the Battle of Bannockburn. The Scots won despite the fact that the English had a highly trained army and were determined on revenge, largely because of the assistance they received from the Knights Templar and Sir William St.Clair and his two sons. The Knights Templar were temporarily secure in Scotland, but clearly the country did not offer the kind of long term security they sought. That security would come in the form of another St.Clair, Henry, born in 1345.

This Henry St. Clair or Sinclair, also known as Henry the Holy, was chosen, after reaching adulthood, leader of an expedition to the New World where the order of Knights Templar could take root. And so they set sail in 1395, years before Columbus, their fleet commanded by Antonio Zeno, brother of the most famous Venetian admiral of the day. Zeno did something else, which if true, has present day implications. It is said that he brought to St. Clair the design of the first cannons used on the Venetian ships.

Off they sailed, Antonio Zeno, Captain and navigator, St. Clair and his friends on a dozen barks with between two and three hundred men, searching for the New World. Along with a map Zeno made was also the ship's log, the so-called "Zeno Narrative".

The Zeno Narrative provides only a general description of the voyage. There are gaps. However, it suggests that they wanted to land in Newfoundland but were driven off by unfriendly natives. Then they came to Chedabucto Bay and dropped anchor in Guysborough Harbour at the beginning of June, 1398. They had seen smoke from a great fire and later detective work and archeology has deduced that it came from an area of asphalt at Stellarton about fifty miles from Guysborough Harbour. They also saw Indians, now presumed to be Mi'kmaq, living in caves in the area.

The story goes that Prince Henry stayed in Nova Scotia and persuaded the Indians to act as his guide while he explored this new territory, while Zeno returned to Europe taking with him his map and log book which were discovered in Venice years later. The following spring the explorers headed south along the coast. It was then that one of the knights, Sir James Gunn, died near what is now the town of Westford in Massachusetts. Many believe that he was buried beside a rock ledge there and an inscription was punched into the stone to commemorate his death. The image, and it can be seen today, is of a Scottish knight with long sword and shield and the Gunn family insignia. Recently, an historian in Westford has erected a monument there. It reads,

Prince Henry First Sinclair of Orkney born in Scotland made a voyage of discovery to North America in 1398. After wintering in Nova Scotia he sailed to Massachusetts and on an inland expedition in 1399 to Prospect Hill to view the surrounding countryside, one of the party died. The punch-hole armorial effigy that adorns this ledge is a Memorial to this Knight.

The Zeno map and narrative has spawned much speculation when they were found in the middle of the sixteenth century. Some associate parts of the narrative with Oak Island, others connect Prince Henry and his men with the Glooscap legend. There are even those who believe that these Knights Templar brought the Holy Grail to Nova Scotia with them.

But what is the Cape Breton connection?

It came much later. Captain George Burchell of Sydney anchored his schooner in Louisbourg Harbour in 1880. When he pulled up this anchor he brought up with it what was thought at first to be a sixteenth century breech loading swivel gun, sometimes called a serpentine gun. It was speculated at the time that it might be of Portuguese origin. Captain Burchell lent it to the Provincial Museum in Halifax but when the Louisbourg Museum was built in 1936 it was taken there. The gun, now on display at Louisbourg Fortress, is about five feet long, composed of bars of forged iron bound together by iron bands.

What vessel would have carried a breech-loading swivel gun? Not a fishing boat, at that time. It is reasonable to conclude that it was either from a warship of some sort or from a colonizing boat. Cape Breton historian J.G. Bourinot wrote that the gun was, despite corrosion, in excellent condition and speculates on the theory that it might have come from one of Sir Humphrey Gilbert's ships, perhaps the one lost off Cape Breton when his fleet was returning from Newfoundland in 1583. However, he dismisses this as unlikely.

According to a letter from the Royal Armouries in Britain this type of gun was introduced around the middle of the sixteenth century and suggested "until we have further evidence it is unwise to date them earlier". But English King Henry VII (late fifteenth century) describes, "Serpentynes of yron in the forecastell aboue the Dekke yche of them with his minches and forloke of yron".

Lack of conclusive proof does not deter speculative historical inquiry. According to Anne Campbell Dixon, the canon has been identified as fourteenth century Venetian, giving it a link to the Zeno brothers. Detractors will argue that even if this gun is fourteenth century, they were very durable and could have been used as late as the sixteenth century or even later and lost overboard then. The French did not occupy Louisbourg until the early eighteenth century! Did it come a British military vessel? According to Tower of London authorities "serpentines", although listed as being used in fortifications, none are listed as being used on the King's ships by 1569.

The answers to three questions need be found. Were the Venetians using guns such as the one found in Louisbourg Harbour in the fourteenth century? Were such guns in use very much later? And if the gun was not from the St. Clair expedition from whom might it have come?

Andrew Sinclair, the former Cambridge academic who has written on the life and exploits of Prince Henry St. Clair and has made a television film for the British Broadcasting Corporation on the topic, believes that the gun at Louisbourg is from the Prince's expedition and that he explored the whole of Nova Scotia and the coast of New England as far south as Rhode Island. He further believes, unlike earlier historical speculation, that the smoke reported in the Zeno Narrative was coming not from burning pitch at Stellarton but burning coal deposits on Cape Breton, and that the smoking hill may have been a distantly seen Cape Smokey.

Historical speculation is stimulating and enjoyable and it would be delightful to find firm evidence that well before Columbus reached the New World a Scotsman found Cape Breton. Alex Storm, historian and archeologist at Louisbourg, while certainly not endorsing the view that Henry St. Clair landed here, did add "we have found Viking remains of a small village (in Newfoundland) from around the year 1100. If a group in 1100 can get here, it would not surprise me if the Scots turned up three hundred years later."

LORD OCHILTREE, THE FIRST CAPE BRETONER

The leader of the first confirmed settlement of pioneers on the shore of Cape Breton was Scotsman, Sir James Stewart, Lord Ochiltree. The settlement lasted just a couple of months in the year 1629 and it is natural to wonder what inspired this Scottish lord to undertake so perilous a journey. In part it was the adventurous climate of the times. The Dutch were in New Amsterdam, now New York. The Pilgrims had landed at Plymouth Rock nine years earlier and the first settlement at Boston was only a year away. In North America there was a New Spain, a New France and a New England. In part it may have been genetic. Lord Ochiltree's father, also named James Stewart, had had a dramatic military career fighting with the Dutch forces in Holland and a political career of plot and counter plot of Byzantine proportions in sixteenth century Scotland. Indeed, Ochiltree's father, though one-time influential in the court of James VI, was assassinated in 1595 and "his head carried in triumph on the point of a spear through the country, while his body was left a prey to the dogs and swine". It may have been prompted by the violence of the times in Scotland but it was most likely the influence of Sir William Alexander, poet, politician and courtier, who dreamed of a landed gentry developing a new Scotland.

In 1621 when Lord Ochiltree was probably in his late thirties or early forties, Sir William received a grant of land in the New World. The charter was written in Latin and so his New Scotland was written as Nova Scotia but it was not until eight years later that the settlers arrived. His grant included all that is now Nova Scotia and New Brunswick and parts of the state of Maine and the province of Quebec. Although James, as King of Scotland made the grants, he laid claim to it as King of England, by right of discovery, thanks to John Cabot in 1497. He was given the right to the revenue from all the natural resources – except the royalty on gold and silver which was to be paid to the crown – could settle the land, establish municipalities, create ports and tariffs. He could administer justice and coin money and his settlers were to enjoy all the liberties of free and native subjects of Scotland.

William Alexander was born about 1567 in the village of Menstrie, near Stirling in south-central Scotland. His father died in 1581 and he succeeded to the title becoming the sixth Baron of Menstrie and, raised by a great uncle attended the local grammar school before entering university, probably at Glasgow and later at Lieden.

It was an adventurous age. The splendor of Queen Elizabeth's years had not long passed and the chivalry of men like Sidney and Raleigh touched an imagination given zest by names such as Drake and Gilbert. For men with a literary taste, such as William Alexander, the influence of Milton and Shakespeare was dominant.

It was on leaving university that a taste for travel may have developed. He set off after his graduation to travel France, Spain and

Italy in the company of his friend and neighbor Archibald, the Earl of Argyll, who later introduced him to King James VI of Scotland. The Court attracted William and he was to remain there for forty years – in Scotland and England for James VI of Scotland became James I of England.

In 1601 he married Janet, the daughter of Sir William Erskine, and she produced eleven children for him. Two years after their marriage the couple moved south to London in the entourage of King James, now king of both Scotland and England. But William Alexander was not simply a family man or a courtier. He was a romantic and a poet. Not one that is remembered today, but his writing was considered a worthy pursuit even though it did not excite the critics - one wrote that none of his poetry "stirred the hearts of his countrymen." His commercial endeavors were not successful either. The king gave him the grant of a silver mine in Scotland but neither he nor the king gleaned profit from it.

Sir William, for all his romantic notions, did have a streak of realism. He wanted to colonize what is now eastern Canada but had no plans to actually go there himself. That was a task for hotter heads. In 1622 he hired a ship in London in the hope of recruiting emigrants, but his vision of a feudal colony where only the landed gentry had a right to purchase land had little appeal for the artisans and farmers he wanted to induce. The handful of settlers that did leave only made it as far as Newfoundland and most of those who did not die during the first winter joined the crews of fishing vessels and made it back the following year to Europe.

Another scheme was needed. King James had devised a method of making money that might be usefully copied by Alexander. The King sold titles, an order of knights baronet who would receive this honour by paying a substantial amount into the royal coffers. They were then proclaimed "Baronets of Ulster". Alexander put it to the king that the colonization of Nova Scotia could similarly become a reality by creating "Baronets of New Scotland". In addition to paying for this title the prospective baronets had also to provide six male colonists, clothed, armed and victualed. For this they would each receive six square miles of Nova Scotia. There were no takers in Scotland. Then another setback. The king died.

The setback was only temporary. The new King, Charles, manipulated the arrangement so that the new titles would be granted not simply by Sir William but by Charles 1, the sovereign, and the offer was open not just to Scots but anyone with the money in Britain. But the French had their eyes on the area as well and were pressing their claims to jurisdiction over New France and Acadia. In 1627 another war broke out between England and France. Undeterred by war, in fact somewhat encouraged by early success against the French, Sir William Alexander put his son, Sir William junior, in command of a colonizing expedition. Accompanying him was Lord Ochiltree (Sir James Stewart, son of the Earl of Arran) who equipped two small ships and recruited sixty settlers to join the expedition. Their vessels were under the command of and escorted by a Captain Kirke, who had achieved success against the French the year before.

In July of 1629 the emigrant ships sailed into Baleine Harbour, so named because of a rock there resembling a whale, the word "baleine" is French for whale. Kirke left them there and sailed on up the St. Lawrence for a further crack at the French. Ochiltree and his settlers at once set to the task of clearing land and building a fort. Sir William junior assisted but he had his own plans and soon set off for Port Royal in mainland Nova Scotia, where he too cleared land and built a built a fort.

Ochiltree and his settlers made a valiant effort but became victims of the war between England and France. A month or so after Ochiltree had landed at Baleine a French Captain Charles Daniel of the Company of New France established his settlement at Great Cibou, now St Ann's Bay, with a garrison of soldiers. He marched against the Scotsmen and captured the lot. Soon the Scottish pioneers were prisoners in St Ann's helping build the fort there. After that they were on their way back to Europe, some to a brief prison term in France but most to the fishing port of Falmouth in southern England. Considering what may have become of them during a winter on the Cape Breton shore at Baleine it was perhaps not so terrible a conclusion to their dreams.

Lord Ochiltree vanished into the pages of history and the title, "Earls of Arran" became extinct in Scotland. In 1762 a title of Irish earls was created, associated with the Arran Isles off Galway and having no connection with the Scottish earldom.

And Sir William Alexander, senior, whose dreams of empire had inspired the adventure? In 1631 he was made sole printer of King James VI and I's version of the Psalms and created Earl of Stirling. But he died insolvent in London in 1640. His poetry is forgotten but the name he gave to his lands in North America is not.

"LORD JEFFREY AMHERST WAS A SOLDIER OF THE KING."

In the early years of the Seven Years' War in Europe the career of Major General Jeffrey Amherst was nondescript, hardly promising. All changed when Secretary of State, William Pitt, believing that the decisive battles would be fought in North America and recognizing Amherst's potential, sent him across the Atlantic to command. His first challenge to French dominance in Canada would be the Fortress of Louisbourg.

As the British army, under Jeffrey Amherst's overall command, positioned to land at Louisbourg in 1758, aboard the ships were all the accoutrements of war, all the bags and baggage that would allow them to lay siege to Louisbourg; arms and ammunition, food and water containers, tents, basic medical supplies and the like, though Amherst was said to be economical with everything except time. But there was one additional element going ashore. It was in the hearts and minds of the soldiers. It was memory of honour abused and it was that memory that not only affected the outcome of the siege but set a pattern that would erode familiar concepts of honourable warfare in the years ahead.

A generation or so later the Duke of Wellington remarked that the British Army was composed of "the scum of the earth". Wellington had a droll tongue and probably intended less than was said. But by the time Wellington fought Napoleon warfare had changed from the days five decades earlier when Amherst and Wolfe faced the regiments under Drucour on Cape Breton. War had become more brutal. War called for short and sharp violence; the total destruction of the enemy. In the words of Wellington before Waterloo, "Hard pounding this, gentlemen; let's see who will pound longest." Fifty-seven years earlier the wife of the governor of Louisbourg, Madame Drucour, received from Lord Amherst, under flag of truce some pineapples as a gift. She responded by sending back to the British lines a few bottles of champagne. Civilized exchanges between combatants was part of the etiquette of warfare. Yet it was at Louisbourg that, despite the pineapples and champagne, these etiquettes began to erode. Why?

When the French surrendered Louisbourg , after the second siege, the forces under Amherst consciously and deliberately refused them the so-called "honours of war". By this practice defeated soldiers were allowed, provided they had given a spirited defense, to march out of their fortress drums beating, side-arms retained and colours flying. This was a practice firmly entrenched among officers on both sides and also, though not widely realized today perhaps because of Wellington's aphorism, among the ordinary soldiers.

Members of the officer class in both the French and the British armies had a highly honed sense of honour and came from the upper classes of their societies. In the French Army the officer class included not only the wealthy aristocracy but also minor and impoverished nobility – as well as bourgeoisie aspiring to the ranks of nobility. There were at that time close to eighty thousand noble families of varying status in France. With this ménage probably came an inclination to over value the superficial attributes of authority, a touchy demand for respect and a concern, possibly obsessive, for the symbols of honour. Military prowess ranked less high. It was written at that time, "a man in the French Army is esteemed an officer so long as he dances, has a nice figure, and is a swordsman". Nevertheless, many of these officers, whatever their technical proficiency, were brave and knew how to face death well.

British Army officers also generally came from the upper classes of society but it was a society far more porous than that of France. In Britain, unlike in continental Europe, there was no legal caste of nobility and only the few hundred members of the peerage, who sat in the House of Lords, could pass their titles onto eldest sons. Their other sons, because of the laws of primogeniture, generally had to enter an array of professions, and some had to earn their living as soldiers, sailors, lawyers, the church or wherever opportunity arose. They were a part of the multi-faceted middle classes and in the rural areas particularly, mixed widely with others as any reader of Jane Austin will recognize. The difference between the two military societies facing each other at Louisbourg is mirrored in their commanding officers. The Governor of Louisbourg was a Norman nobleman, the Chevalier Augustin de Drucour. Facing him was Major General Jeffrey Amherst. He did not become a member of the peerage until after the campaign. Amherst's father's income came from his revenues from his land, his earnings as a lawyer and revenue from London property, which included a tavern.

The backbone of the two armies, the other ranks and non-commissioned officers had more in common. Their attitudes towards

North America might have been different. The authorities in Britain had long been expansionist, viewed emigration to North America favourably. France wanted to keep its people at home, to fill the ranks of its enormous army. Charles Maurice de Talleyrand, looking bitterly back fifty years with the benefit of hindsight, said America was a place for "individuals without industry, without leaders and without morals". But both the British and French soldiers were largely from the labouring classes and the indigent. Despite the harsh punishments of the day they regarded their regiment as their family and their loyalty was to that family. In both armies that loyalty was enhanced by visible symbols, in particular the regimental colours.

Over the generations these colours were initially the means by which the ordinary soldier could identify the rallying point of his regiment despite the confusion of battle. Gradually they acquired an almost mystical significance embodying loyalty to the crown and pride in the achievements of the regiment. In the case of French regiments colours symbolized loyalty to the king and were emblazoned with the fleur de lys. Among the men of the older established French regiments at Louisbourg, the Artois, the Burgundians and the Cambris, the intensity of emotion they evoked would probably have been more intense than the Canadian-raised Marine regiments. British regiments had two colours, the regimental, emblazoned with battle honours, and the king's and the attitude towards them is probably summed up in some words written more than a century later.

> A moth eaten rag on a worm-eaten pole
> It does not look likely, to stir a man's soul
> 'Tis the deeds that were done 'neath the moth-eaten rag
> When the pole was a staff and the rag was a flag.

Both Amherst and Drucour, their officers and men, would have shared the sentiment of Shakespeare's King Henry that, "if it be a sin to covet honour, I am the most offending soul alive".

The details of the siege of Louisbourg are fully described elsewhere. The French fought valiantly. Once their re-supply routes were cut off by both land and sea, defeat was inevitable. Amherst controlled the approaches by land, Admiral Boscowen and his fleet the entrance to Louisbourg Harbour. Once Boscowen had destroyed the French warships in the harbour under the command of Admiral des Gouttes, the final collapse of the fortress was inevitable.

What is often not dwelt upon are the final hours. Drucour sent General Amherst a request for an honourable capitulation, one that acknowledged that the garrison had fought with honour and the officers had conducted the defense with gallantry. There were years of precedent for this.

Ten years earlier, British troops had gone into winter quarters at Grand Pre on the mainland of Nova Scotia. In a daring raid the French had overwhelmed the British after more than half their number were dead or wounded. The British were promised the honours of war and on the evening of the surrender the Frenchmen were formally invited to drinks and dinner and a convivial evening was passed. The following day the British marched out on their way to Annapolis Royal, muskets at the shoulder, drums beating, colours flying. Two years prior to Louisbourg the same courtesy was accorded to the British who surrendered after the battle of Minorca, the island in the Mediterranean. Tradition demanded it. The custom of siege warfare was that when the attacking force breached the walls or when further opposition was hopeless, the inhabitants would be asked to surrender. If they agreed satisfactory terms were usually reached particularly if the defense had been vigorous. Included in the surrender terms would be the right of the defeated to the honours of war. If, on the other hand, the defenders did not surrender the attackers had to storm the breach and fight their way in neither the garrison nor the civilian inhabitants could expect mercy. The cry of "No quarter" would be heard.

Drucour offered to surrender. He wanted and asked for an honourable capitulation. Amherst retorted that he demanded unconditional surrender, one without the honours of war, and he gave Drucour one hour in which to comply or face the consequences. The French military were appalled. They prepared to dig in and fight to the finish. The senior civil official feared the consequences of resistance and appealed to Drucour to change his mind for fear that a general assault would result in the cry of "No quarter", and that the civilians would suffer.

Drucour reluctantly informed the British that he would surrender unconditionally. The civilian population was undoubtedly relieved. But not the military. Officers of the Cambris Regiment were "filled with indignation, tore up their colours, and each soldier, in imitation of them, took his musket by one end and, striking the butt, smashed it to pieces". The men in the ranks took the remains of the colours and, so that the British would not have them, set them alight. In the early hours of 27 July 1758, the formal surrender took place. The remaining colours were surrendered and the soldiers of the garrison "threw their arms on the ground and turned away, weeping".

The question must be; why did the British inflict this humiliation on the French?

The answer lies in the recent memories of the British officers and their men, memories that would help explain a reported incident on the day General Wolfe and his men landed at Kenington Cove a few miles south of Louisbourg. A British naval officer examining the abandoned French outposts between the Cove and the fortress found "the Bodies of one hundred and odd French regulars and two Indians which our Rangers scalped". Why scalped and not simply killed? Many of the Rangers were from Massachusetts and men from Massachusetts remembered the horrifying tales – undoubtedly embellished but widely believed – of what had happened to Massachusetts's men after the siege of Fort William Henry less than a year before.

At Fort William Henry French General Montcalm, later to die with Wolfe at Quebec, lay siege to British forces commanded by Colonel George Monro. In the fort were five companies of the 35th Foot along with two independent New York companies and nearly eight hundred provincial militiamen from New Jersey and New Hampshire. Serving with Montcalm were hundreds of Indians. Monro sent out by boat a reconnaissance-in-force. It was ambushed. Reported Montcalm's aide de camp, the Indians

> Brought back nearly two hundred prisoners, the rest were drowned. The Indians jumped into the water and speared them like fish… The rum which was in the barges and which the Indians immediately drank caused them to commit great cruelties. They put in the pot and ate three prisoners and perhaps others were so treated. All have become slaves unless they are ransomed. A horrible spectacle to European eyes.

Monro, his force now severely depleted, desperately needed more men. He received two hundred regulars of the Royal American (60th) Regiment – who, nine months later would be in Louisbourg – and eight hundred Massachusetts provincials. No sooner had they arrived than Montcalm's besieging force closed on them. They numbered more than four thousand and included one thousand five hundred Indians. After a week Monro had to accept Montcalm's terms. They were honourable ones that acknowledged that Monro had resisted according to the highest military standards. The entire garrison would be granted safe passage, allowed to keep its personal possessions and side arms and march out, colours flying and hauling a symbolic fieldpiece. The sick and wounded would stay in the fort protected by the French.

Unfortunately the French had not consulted their Indian allies when arranging these terms that did not conform to Indian concepts of warfare. The Indians wanted rewards for their contribution to the siege. As soon as the British left the Indians entered the fort and many of the wounded prisoners were scalped despite French efforts to protect them. Monro's men, marching out, were protected at the head by French troops, but the provincials, principally men from Massachusetts and the women and children camp followers were not. The Indians set upon them. In minutes, close to two hundred had been killed and scalped and as many as five hundred taken captive to be ransomed later. One was ritually eaten by Indians after he had been taken north to Montreal.

Over the next week the survivors, including Monro and the symbolic canon, reached British lines. But news of the massacre spread throughout the American colonies. Certainly Montcalm tried to prevent the massacre. That so many of the surrendered garrison had been murdered even though their safety had been guaranteed would reflect upon Montcalm's own honour. More immediately he must have realized that the British, when their time came, would not be disposed to treat the French so honourably.

Other events, recorded around Lunenbourg in Nova Scotia fueled the anathema towards Indians at that time. Colonists there with their wives and children were shot and scalped and kidnapped.

Unlike Wolfe, who was known for his unrestrained comments about Indians, Amherst was not vocal in his condemnation. His actions spoke for him. Drucour and his men were a part of that same army that had failed to prevent the massacre at Fort William Henry the previous year. By his friends and allies would he be judged. They would not march out of Louisbourg with colours flying and drums beating. They would sleep in the streets and doorways of the defeated town until shipped back to France. And for the rest of Amherst's career he would continue to deny the honours of war to any defeated French force. More than that, the French civilians would be shipped out as well. No longer were only the soldiers the enemy. On Cape Breton Island Amherst's refusal to play the magnanimous victor was an early sign of impending total war.

Governor Drucour, his officers and men and the civilians of the fortress returned to France. Admiral De Gouttes paid for the defeat. His patent of nobility was burned by the common hangman and he was sentenced to twenty one years in prison.

The fortress itself was totally destroyed under the direction of "Foul Weather Jack" Byron grandfather of the English poet.

Montcalm died on the Heights of Abraham in Quebec as did British General Wolfe who had been subordinate to Amherst at Louisbourg..

Amherst went on to further success, at the Battle of Ticonderoga and the capture of Montreal, though his antipathy towards Indians may have caused the Pontiac Rebellion. He was appointed Governor General of British possessions in America. In 1776 he was raised to the peerage as Baron Amherst of Montreal. He died in England in 1797 at his home named "Montreal". But it was Louisbourg that made him.

ENSIGN PRENTIES – SURVIVOR

Samuel Walter Prenties didn't mean to arrive on Cape Breton. An Ensign in the 84th Regiment of Foot, he was on a mission, carrying important dispatches from the British forces at Quebec to Sir Henry Clinton in New York during the American Revolutionary War.

Originally from Ireland, the Prenties family were now successful innkeepers in Quebec City. The father, Miles, had been a Provost Marshall in Wolfe's army and had fought together with Richard Montgomery years before against the French at Louisbourg and later on the Plains of Abraham.

Now on opposing sides, Montgomery and the rebel Americans, recently successful in capturing Montreal from the British, were advancing on Quebec City. Faced with yet more rebels under Benedict Arnold coming from the south, Quebec City was vulnerable.

Experienced veterans of the Royal Highland Emigrants formed the core of the new 84th Regiment of Foot. Many had also fought years before with Wolfe against the French. Recruits were sought. They had to be "17 years or more, (drummers could be younger), at least

5'3", appear healthy, have all limbs, no ruptures, not troubled by fits, and have at least 2 teeth that met." Samuel, just over twenty, and his younger brother fit the bill. The American attack on New Year's Eve was their first battle. The City held its own. With the retreating American armies, Canada remained in British hands.

Prenties purchased his commission in 1778, but he was not a gung-ho soldier. A scrappy young man he tried his best to avoid soldiering with his Regiment, usually complaining of ill health. In light of what followed this claim seems unlikely to be true.

He left Quebec on 17 November, 1780 aboard the brig the *St. Lawrence*. Not long afterwards the *St Lawrence* was caught in a heavy snowstorm, her rigging caked with ice and the seams of her hull, opened by the storm, were being desperately caulked with small chunks of beef. On 5 December just off the west coast of Cape Breton, the brig began to founder. That was only the beginning of the problems. The Captain was drunk and kept to his bunk and Prenties had to bribe the crew with wine to get them to keep the pumps working. But the brig finally ran aground.

Ensign Prenties reached shore with his servant, two sailors, the mate and a boy passenger, who died in the night. Their clothing was frozen. There was no food or fire. They pushed their way through waist high snow to the shelter of nearby woods, some two hundred and fifty yards away. Prenties and the mate were forced to beat their companions with branches to keep them from falling asleep and dying.

At daylight the following day, the survivors on land helped the men still on the boat to shore. The storm continued six more days. By then the survivors had saved what they could from the wreck including some onions and salt beef and they had made a roofless shelter out of planking.

Leaving a small group behind, on 4 January, 1781, Prenties, his servant, the useless Captain, the mate and two sailors set out northward in a patched up lifeboat to find "civilization". They had a few supplies, including some beef, onions and means for making fires. Soon even trying to get firewood was too much of an effort.

They clung to the coastline, sometimes being held up for days by storms. At one point they found remains of summer fishing huts, but no supplies and no people. Persevering on, they traveled some one hundred and forty miles around the northern tip of Cape Breton. The boat sprung more leaks. The survivors had oakum but no pitch to bind it. Prenties threw water on the oakum hoping it would freeze and stop up the leaks. By the middle of February the survivors had reached the area of St Ann's Bay. Supplies had run out and there had been discussion about choosing lots to see who would be sacrificed so the others could survive. Now completely exhausted and in a dreadful state, they were existing on boiled kelp and melted mutton tallow candles, which made them violently ill.

By chance, two Mi'kmaq hunters discovered them near death, gave them food and built a roaring fire. The Mi'kmaq returned shortly afterwards and took the group further inland up the Bay to their winter camp at Goose Cove. Here an old woman remembered the survivors of another shipwreck, *L'Auguste* off Cape North some twenty years earlier. By a strange coincidence the Mi'kmaq who was translating for the present survivors had rescued the Captain of *L'Auguste*.

If, after they had been shipwrecked, Prenties and the other survivors had turned south instead of north, they would have reached "civilization" at St Peters within about two days and have been spared their extreme hardships.

Mi'kmaq went overland to rescue the others left behind. Not all had survived. The group now followed guides around and through the Bras d'Or Lakes to St Peters. Getting on to Halifax and then onto New York took more time as American privateers were ravaging along the coastline.

In August, some nine months after he had left Quebec, Prenties finally arrived in New York and delivered his dispatches. Duty done.

Afterwards Prenties traveled to England where he had published a narrative account of his ordeal. A review of <u>A Castaway on Cape Breton</u> in the *London Review* (Vol. 67, 1782) was not kind.

"This narrative contains little that can amuse any reader. The incidents are told with coldness. The author can neither instruct nor please. The matter is often vulgar, sometimes silly and always insipid. The performance will be opened without anxiety, and thrown away with disgust." In spite of this review, the book was successful and five editions were published.

Prenties returned to Canada, purchased a lieutenancy in the 84th, and continued to be at odds with the military. Later he and his brother established a fishing business in the Gaspe area, and later on the Miramachi.

LAW AND ORDER – EARLY CAPE BRETON

A man steals some clothing. He's caught, brought to trial and sentenced. His sentence is the first one passed down by the Supreme Court of Cape Breton. But, did the punishment fit the crime?

In the late fall of 1784 two groups of settlers arrived on the newly formed Colony of Cape Breton. DesBarres and his English settlers spent the first winter in the old barracks protecting the coalmines at what is now Sydney Mines. The group of Loyalists accompanying Abraham Cuyler, the former mayor of Albany, New York, spent what must have been a miserable first winter in the scattered fishing huts and ruins of the French fortress at Louisbourg. Come the spring, everyone would be together at the newly established capital, Sydney.

But when in Louisbourg a man had stolen from Jonathan Jones' store "Sixteen pairs of white yarn stockings of the value of eight shillings; eight check shirts to the value of twelve shillings, and two pairs of cloth breeches to the value of two shillings." On 2 November

1785 the thief was brought before the newly formed Supreme Court of Cape Breton.

The trial of this unknown felon took place in February where he was found guilty. In the formality of those days he was then asked what he could say why sentence of death should not be pronounced. The man pleaded "Benefit of Clergy", which was allowed. The sentence was reduced and he was ordered to be burned on the hand and to work for six months "in His Majesty's mines at Spanish River"(Sydney Harbour). Shortly afterwards two brothers also accused of theft received similar punishment.

Pleading "Benefit of Clergy" was a long established custom that mitigated the harsher penalties of law. The contrivance dated from early medieval years when the clergy, generally people who could read and write, had their own laws in an ecclesiastical court usually less savaged than legal punishment suffered by others. Over the generations it had strayed from its original intent and its later use derived from the linguistic connection between the word "clerk" and "cleric". So when a prisoner pleaded "Benefit of Clergy" he or she had to be able to read aloud the first verse of the fifty-first psalm, known as "the Neck Verse". This read, "Have mercy upon me, O God, according to thy loving kindness: according unto the multitude of they tender mercies blot out my transgressions." If the prisoner could read this it could be formally said, "Legit ut clericus" or "he (or she) reads like a clerk" and the neck would be spared. Later, for lesser offenses the punishment would be less draconian. Later still the more serious crimes were excluded and "Benefit of Clergy" was finally abolished in 1827. In England in the 1780's, despite the myriad of crimes for which the death penalty could be imposed, there was only an average of fifty- six executions a year. In the early part of the nineteenth century between 1806 and 1827, some

4,126 people were sentenced to death but only 536 executions were carried out.

Punishments continued to be harsh but not ultimate. After the survivors of their first winter in Louisbourg moved to Sydney to join the British immigrants records of crime and punishment are sparse. However, on 15 July 1801 another man was indicted for grand larceny. Again, the prisoner was asked if he had anything to say why sentence of death should not be passed on him. He replied that he is a clerk and prayed for "Benefit of Clergy". This was granted and the court sentenced that "he be whipped until his back be bloody from the goal (jail) door along the street called Charlotte Street to the house of Thomas LeCras, (at the corner of Nepean Street) from thence down the street to the Esplanade and along the Esplanade (the street parallel to the water) to the house of the Honourable Richard Stout (at the corner of Esplanade and DesBarres) and thence to the goal door; and that he undergo six months imprisonment and costs." - rather a painful tour of the town as it was at that time.

But what if a man could not plead "Benefit"? The legend is that there was a man who either did not or could not so plead. He had drunk too much – liquor flowed liberally in those early days in Sydney – when he came to a house where a pane of glass was missing and had been stuffed with clothing to keep out the cold. The clothing included a man's coat, which the drunken wanderer found fitted him. He took it. A few days later he was arrested when the owner identified the coat as her own. He found guilty and sentenced to death. The community was horrified but the law being the law it must be carried out. A petition for clemency was widely circulated and quickly signed. Eventually a response was received, the criminal pardoned and released.

Sydney boasted a public whipping post and the Stocks, "a framework with holes for securing the ankles and sometimes the wrists, used to expose an offender to public derision". This was popular. But the public flogging of a felon through the streets remained equally as popular. These punishments were usually followed by imprisonment for theft and even for habitual drunkenness but what must be the most interesting criminal case in early Sydney was handled by Judge John George Marshall, son of a Loyalist.

In 1823, after a distinguished legal career he was appointed Chief Justice for the County of Cape Breton, which in those days covered the entire island. That same year a prisoner was convicted before him of "the very worst description on the person of a female", presumably rape. The Judge sentenced him to two years imprisonment in Halifax and he was put aboard a collier bound there. The prisoner was held in irons with two armed guards and the collier set sail. Its first stop was to pick up coal about nine miles from Sydney. At that point forty miners, their faces disguised, stormed the ship, seized the guards and carried the prisoner to a nearby blacksmith's shop where his irons were struck off. He disappeared and was never captured again. Remarked the judge, "in other parts of the island at that time there were not a few others of the same lawless disposition".

WYNYARD AND THE 33RD

There have been barracks at the north end of Sydney since the community was first established in 1785. Today the modern facilities hardly distinguish them from many other government erected facilities and they have replaced the somewhat doleful barracks that existed until a few years ago. Since the last British troops were withdrawn at the time of the Crimean War the barracks have been the home of local militia units and have had little impact on the lives of the majority of Cape Bretoners. It was not always so.

The first troops, officers and men of the 33rd Regiment, were commanded by the irascible Colonel Yorke and stationed in Sydney following the arrival of the Loyalists from the former American colonies and immigrant Englishmen who had crossed the Atlantic with Governor DesBarres' group.

The regiment had suffered hard times. Eight years earlier they had left their barracks in Ireland, where they had been stationed through most of the years of the Seven Years' War and the decade that followed, and landed at Charleston in South Carolina in the summer of 1776. At this time the 33rd was highly regarded in the British Army. Wrote a

Roger Lamb, a Sergeant in the 23rd Royal Welch Fusiliers, " I am bound to report here that I have felt a certain shamefacedness on visiting the barracks of the 33rd Regiment, who were commanded by the young Earl of Cornwallis, to compare their high state of appointment and steadiness of their discipline with the slovenly and relaxed bearing of most of our own companies." Major General William Howe wrote, the 33rd's drill and discipline is "established upon the truest principles, Far Superior to any other Corps within my observation."

Shortly after the regiment participated in the Battle of Long Island – which lost General Washington New York City – and in numerous actions, ranging from the battle of Brandywine to the siege of Charleston and culminating in the battle of Yorktown that ended with the surrender of the army under Cornwallis. The surrender meant the temporary disintegration of the 33rd. Gradually the survivors came together again in New York and finally, then under the command of Lt Colonel Yorke who had been their commander at Yorktown, they headed for Sydney. According to one historical report they had few provisions or adequate clothing and many died on their way. Some senior officers, including their Colonel, Earl Cornwallis, and Captain Frederick Cornwallis, had avoided this posting and been sent straight to England. It was a shattered and demoralized regiment that began work in Sydney by building its own barracks. Their commanding officer, Yorke, determined to shape them again into the prestigious formation they had once been and in so doing earned for himself a reputation of cantankerous disciplinarian.

This was a rancorous period throughout Nova Scotia and the newly formed Cape Breton colony. Loyalists, many of whom had surrendered everything save their principles when fleeing north, were often at loggerheads with officers of the garrison. Too often the Loyalist civilians regarded the officers as graceful but useless social appendages while they in turn regarded the town officials as bumptious colonists with few social graces. At formal events the two groups of society enjoyed each other's company, particularly since junior officers could not have wives and some colonial officials had daughters. Outside of these events both groups tended to keep to themselves.

Consequently it was not unusual for two young officers, Captain John Cope Sherbrooke and Lieutenant George Wynyard to eat in the barracks then sit reading in their rooms. Sherbrooke and Wynyard were doing just this in the fall of 1785. They had arrived only a few months before and what little entertainment they found in town had either been exhausted or found wanting; both came from military families and their future service gives nothing to suggest that either of them were unusually frivolous. By 1811 Sherbrooke had been knighted and was appointed Governor of Nova Scotia; still later, following the War of 1812, Lord Sherbrooke became Governor-General of Canada. Wynyard would rise to the rank of Lieutenant Colonel and command the 24th Light Dragoons. Lord Cornwallis, their former commander, returned to England where he was appointed Governor General of India.

On 15 October, 1785, Sherbrooke and Wynyard ate an early meal in Wynyard's quarters. No wine or liquor was served with the meal. Their dining room had two doors, one leading to a passage, the other to Wynyard's bedroom. The bedroom had only one window and it was sealed tight for the winter with putty.

Some movement caused Sherbrooke to glance up. To his surprise, standing at the doorway to the passage was a young man, about twenty years old, who looked very ill. Unlike Sherbrooke and Wynyard who were warmly dressed, this newcomer was wearing only very light clothing and had shrunken cheeks and looked half starved. Sherbooke's surprise caused Wynyard to look up as well; his reaction was quite different. He turned white, froze in his seat and said not a word. The young intruder smiled briefly at him, walked across the room and went into Wynyard's bedroom. A moment later, overcoming his surprise, Wynyard jumped up and gasped to Sherbrooke, "That's my brother". The two of them dashed towards the bedroom. There was no one there. The room was quite empty and the window remained sealed.

Wynyard was immediately convinced that what they had seen was the ghost of his brother, John Otto, serving with the Guards in India. Something, he told Sherbrooke, must be terribly wrong. Sherbrooke was far from convinced. The so-called apparition was, he thought, a hoax played on them by brother officers.

A mutual friend, Lieutenant Ralph Gore advised them to say nothing to the others who, if it were a hoax would soon be goaded by their silence to admit it. Wynyard ignored the advice. So agitated was he by what had happened and the foreboding that what he had seen was the ghost of his dead brother, that he told some other friends. Within days the story had spread through Sydney.

A few months later, on 2 February 1786, a Grand Jury foreman, William Brown, told the Supreme Court of Nova Scotia that Sherbrooke and Wynyard should answer for their refusal to allow one of the governor's agents to examine the floors in the living quarters of the barracks and that the officers' servants should be questioned. Clearly, there was considerable speculation in the community and a belief among some that an unpleasant joke had been played. Neither Sherbrooke nor Wynyard would cooperate. Wynyard was upset that it was a sign that his brother was dead and in all probability neither wanted a group of uppity civilians poking around their quarters. Their reaction was probably "Who does this man Brown think he is? Let him and the civil authorities keep their noses out of a purely military concern."

When these events occurred the last boat for England had already left so there was no way for Wynyard or anyone else to send a letter enquiring after John Otto Wynyard. The few ships that arrived had all left England prior to 5 October. It was not until 6 June, 1786, that the first mail arrived from England. There were no letters for Wynyard.

There were, however, letters for Sherbrooke. One of them read, "Dear John, break to your friend Wynyard the death of his favorite brother." Lieutenant John Otto Wynyard, Lieutenant in the 3rd Regiment of Foot Guards, died in India on 15 October, 1785.

The story does not quite end there. Some years later, after his return to England, Sherbrooke was walking down Piccadilly in London when he saw on the opposite side of the street a man bearing a striking resemblance to the figure seen in the Sydney barracks. He crossed the street and spoke to the man, telling him the story of the ghost and expressing his belief that this man must have something to do with it. The stranger had never been out of England, but he was the twin brother of John Otto Wynyard.

DAVID TAITT - SURVEYOR AND INDIAN AGENT

One of the more modest members of Sydney's first executive council, a council fraught with acrimony between the first Loyalist and English settlers, was David Taitt, the colony's first provost marshal. Yet David Taitt, prior to arriving on Cape Breton had a career in the southern colonies of America that would have chilled the blood of his colleagues. Records of his activity in and around Sydney are few. We know that he supported Lieutenant Governor DesBarres in his dispute with Attorney-General David Mathews, we know that he did much of the detailed work drawing up the plans of the new city, we know that he had an estate of about one thousand acres on the Mira River. But the examination of the Sydney records do little to reveal the true character of the man. This is revealed when American historical records from Florida, Alabama and the Carolinas are unearthed.

Young Taitt arrived in Florida from Scotland in 1763 at the age of twenty-four when what could be described as the world's first "world war" fought in the Americas, Europe, India, the Philippines and the

Caribbean, had just ended. This war, the Seven Years War, known in America as the French-Indian War that ended with the Treaty of Paris, transformed North America. France, whose colonial Empire ran from Canada down the Mississippi, lost everything to the British and Spain acquired New Orleans. Thousands of Indians in tribes ranging from the Abenakis in the north to the Chickasaws and Creeks in the south found their old trading arrangements with the French ended.

Initially Taitt arrived in St. Augustine as an assistant surveyor paid thirty pounds a year and was employed in various tasks concerned with laying out roads. Florida, which had been Spanish, was ceded to the British who divided it into two provinces, East and West Florida. The principal European settlements were St. Augustine in the east and Pensacola in the west and there was a degree of prosperity. Taitt had not been long in North America when he became attached to the Indian Department. This department controlled the entire British North America, excluding Hudson's Bay, and was divided into two areas controlled by superintendents, William Johnson in the north, John Stuart in the south. The primary concern of both was to maintain the integrity of the so-called Proclamation Line.

This Line, roughly following the watershed of the Appalachian Mountains, was the point beyond which white settlement should not be permitted since it was reserved for the Indians living to the west of it as far as the Mississippi. It was far from being an easy task. Land hungry settlers avidly eyed the "empty land" beyond the mountains and welcomed any opportunity that enabled them to breach the Line. The Indians too were mistrustful since various land acquisitions beyond the Line, legitimized as long-term leases with the Indians, were surreptitiously converted into purchase agreements. Even when land was sold by Indians with tribal council consent, there could be misunderstanding. The land may have been sold to pay off huge indebtedness to traders, many of whom were dishonest, and the Indians often failed to understand that selling the land meant giving up all rights to it.

In the Indian Territory there were additional aggravations. Prior to the Proclamation a form of frontier rough justice prevailed. Governors approved traders, the sale of rum was limited and a price schedule agreed on, and trade had to be carried on openly in Indian towns, not in the bush. After the Proclamation trade was declared open to all British subjects provided they had a license. To limit the free enterprise of British subjects was contrary to their rights and liberties.

The Indian Department knew which traders were reliable and the job of the Indian agents was to work with the tribes and protect them from the more avaricious. The head of the Southern Indian Department, John Stuart, a personal friend of the Cherokees, had a Cherokee wife who had borne him a son. The Chickasaws were long-standing friends of the English. The Creeks were a worry. David Taitt was sent to them to establish good relations and to report on the economically important deerskin trade. He was also to report on Indian attitudes to ceding blocks of land to the government. There could be advantages to this since affluent settlers, rather than backcountry frontier squatters, could buy the land from the government and be able to build schools, raise militias and erect churches. Taitt was also told to keep his ears and eyes open and discover if any Spanish or French intrigues were fomenting.

John Stuart wrote,

> (Taitt is a)good surveyor and a person of prudence, he will answer the purposes of observing the disposition of the Indians and obtaining some knowledge of their intrigues with

the Spaniards and the western tribes as well as giving a more perfect idea of the geography of the country in which all the printed maps are shamefully defective.

Taitt left Pensacola at the end of January in 1772 accompanied only by an interpreter. In his diary the geography of interior South Carolina, Georgia and the area soon to be named Alabama is detailed as well as his relations with the Indian leaders he met. He writes scathingly of some of the traders and the debilitating affect the rum they supplied was having. One trader he arrested and sent back to Pensacola. After four months travel he arrived in Atlanta and was rewarded by being appointed a Justice of the Peace in the Creek country north of Pensacola and, more importantly, Commissary for the Upper Creek Towns around Little Tallassee.

Over the next four years American discontent with rule from London grew. American anger with the London government placed the interior settlers of the southern colonies in a dilemma. It was all very well for the residents of coastal towns and secured settlements to rage against London but frontier settlers feared an Indian war. Wrote an advertiser in the *Georgia Gazette:*

> Because the persons who are most active on this occasion are those whose property lies in or near Savannah and, therefore, are not immediately exposed to the bad effects of an Indian war; whereas, the back settlements of this province and our Parish in particular would be most certainly laid waste and depopulated unless we receive such powerful aid and assistance as none but Great Britain can give. For these and many other reasons, we declare our dissent to all resolutions

by which His Majesty's favour and protection might be forfeited.

There were reasons for fear. Young Creeks angry at the moves westward of settlers had massacred them. Tension between Indian and whites grew. One evening Taitt, a guest of a wealthy settler who had bought an estate from prominent trader Lachlan McGillivray, sat down to dinner with the family when suddenly nine Creek warriors burst into the house. They intended no harm. Probably led by famed Indian warrior Emistisiguo, they wanted to talk peace. Taitt, a friend of Emistisiguo, quieted the fears of his hosts and marched more than a hundred miles with the intruders and sixty more warriors to Savannah where talks were begun with the governor.

At the outbreak of the Revolutionary War Taitt and other British Indian agents gathered arms and ammunition for the Indians, most of whom supported the British who had been giving them gifts for years. One Indian trader who supported the American revolutionaries was George Galpin and such was Taitt's influence among the Creeks that Galpin arranged to have Taitt assassinated. Fortunately for Taitt, the chief of the Creeks, Alexander McGillivray, was staunchly Loyalist and managed to get him quickly out of the back country and to the safety of Pensacola. Galpin soon lost influence with the Indians since he had few supplies and little money. Furthermore, the back country "patriots" as the rebels were now called, were trying to devise means of annihilating the Indians and their commanding general in the south, Charles Lee, wanted to "exterminate and route these savages out of their nation".

The military commander of the Loyalists in the backcountry was Thomas Brown, a wealthy twenty-four year old Yorkshire man whose lack of experience was offset by his enthusiasm. He had a high regard for Taitt and the other Indian agents. They had, he wrote, "a perfect knowledge of the language, customs, manners and disposition of the different tribes of Creeks and Cherokees (and were) expert woodsmen capable of swimming any river in the province". After a few years of border raiding with his band of Rangers, Brown was appointed to command all Indian agents in the south and soon after Taitt, several hundred Creek warriors and some leading Cherokees, embittered by American destruction of their villages, were heading out of Pensacola overland on their way to attack Augusta, Georgia, and any other targets of opportunity in between.

Indian agents at that time had close relationships with the Indians in their area of responsibility. Like others, Taitt had married a Creek woman of importance, one Sehoy McGillivray, sister of Alexander. Due to the battles ahead Taitt was unaware that Sehoy was pregnant with his child. When Taitt and his party reached Augusta the town had already reverted to British control but word was received that American patriots had besieged Savannah. Taitt and some of the Indians cut through rebel lines and reached the city where they stayed at the plantation of McGillivray's father. There they prepared for the assault by Americans who were supported by a French fleet that had sailed up from the Caribbean. Taitt, who was now given the rank of captain, commanded two pieces of artillery and in the ensuing battle both Americans and French were driven off and suffered heavy casualties.

Taitt remained in Georgia until the fall of 1779 but by then there were new dangers. Spain declared war against Great Britain, probably in hope of retrieving Florida, and soldiers and Indians were needed for the defense of Pensacola, threatened by the troops of the Spanish Governor in New Orleans, Don Bernado de Galvez. Taitt was soon tramping his way back over the hundreds of miles to West Florida where many Loyalist refugees from Georgia had since fled.

Galvez' Spanish troops quickly captured Baton Rouge and then Natchez, giving him control of the lower Mississippi. Then in March, 1780 after a lengthy siege, captured Mobile. Taitt's task at this point was to lead his Indians in harassing attacks on isolated Spanish units and their foraging parties. They were most successful and an enraged Galvez wanted Taitt captured. An expedition was sent out and on 1 June Taitt was captured by the Spanish thirty miles north of Mobile and taken to prison there. Conditions were harsh. He was shackled with a bilboe – a long iron bar with sliding shackles clamped to the prisoners ankles and to the ground – and at least one prisoner, John Stuart's cousin, died in captivity. Only after Taitt gave his word that when paroled he would not incite Indians against the Spanish was he was freed to travel to Pensacola and join the British garrison there.

In the Spring of 1781 Galvez began his attack on Pensacola and after a couple of months it was brought to a dramatic end. One Spanish shell landed in the ammunition dump inside the fort and over one hundred soldiers were killed. The commander, with no ammunition and after such a significant loss of men, had little recourse but to surrender. Galvez took over a thousand British prisoners who were paroled and returned to Britain.

But what of Taitt? There were reports that Taitt, after capture was taken to a Spanish ship but later escaped. Other reports had it that Galvez wanted him executed for breaking parole. Did he then join the Indian agents with the Choctaws and Chickasaws operating with Colonel Thomas Brown around Augusta? Or was he back with the Creeks continuing to prowl around Spanish occupied Pensacola? Whatever speculations, and he may simply have been among the troops heading back to England, it is certain that in 1782 he was in London where he lodged claims with the Loyalist Claims Commission. He also applied for a position in the Indian Department in other British territories, applying for a position as Indian agent in "Senegambia".

He arrived in Sydney, Nova Scotia late in 1784 with Lieutenant Governor J.F.W. DesBarres' group aboard the ship *Blenheim* with the appointment of Provost Marshal to the new colony of Cape Breton. But there is little doubt that his experience as a surveyor was used in those early years on Cape Breton. In May of 1785 he accompanied DesBarres in the initial survey for establishing the new town of Sydney. "in a few days we fixed on this spot, which is one of the pleasantest situations…; fine harbour, where the largest of British ships can go; possibility of great commerce being well situated for the whale and other fisheries." He added that there was much timber available and that "Britain will be repaid in time…provided care is taken to preserve the fishery and coal trade. Tenders is (sic) necessary to preserve the coal (from) being carried off clandestinely and the fishery, by improper behaviour of our Neighbours ruined." Some of his problems ring a sympathetic note today. In laying out the town "I experienced great trouble and fatigue, in the heat of summer, tormented with mosquitoes (sic) and very few to assist me, notwithstanding I have the satisfaction to acquaint you that I have surmounted every difficulty and have the pleasure of seeing buildings daily raising (sic)."

As a member of the executive council he sided with the governor in his dispute with Attorney General David Mathews over the distribution of supplies. This brought him into conflict with Colonel Yorke of the 33rd as well. When the *President* arrived in October 1785 with supplies they were given to Yorke. DesBarres wanted them for the community not just the soldiers and sent Taitt aboard to take possession. Yorke refused to allow Taitt anywhere near them and DesBarres and Taitt had to back off. Then another supply ship, the *Brandywine,* arrived with forty thousand rations. DesBarres was determined to assert his authority and ordered Taitt aboard to take possession of the food. Again he was run off. A compromise was reached and some of the food eventually was handed over to DesBarres. The community was by this time in some turmoil. Des Barres wanted an example made of the soldiers who had blocked Taitt. And a jury wanted them tried for sedition and treason. Excitement grew. Yorke ordered ammunition issued to his soldiers. The Council wanted the riot act read. Taitt was again sent aboard the *Brandywine* and this time a scuffle broke out. "One of the guards gave him (Taitt) a gentle prick with a Bayonet behind, on which he let go and the posse went off." DesBarres wanted the soldiers arrested and Yorke forbade them entering the town for fear of riots between his men and the population. The antagonism between the military and civilians continued until, to DesBarres' relief, the 33rd Regiment was replaced by the 42nd Regiment.

Taitt meanwhile continued in the faction that opposed Mathews in the council and, when in 1795 Mathews became senior councilor, he lost his job of provost marshal. Mathews replaced him with his own son, William Tryon Mathews.

Taitt retired to his farm, one thousand acres on the south side of the Mira River. He served intermittently on the Council for more than twenty years and was a member of the final council that was compelled to accept the annexation of Cape Breton by Nova Scotia. Little is known of his life on the Mira and he eventually retired to Halifax for his final years. He leaves the impression that he was a man of who fought as hard as was possible for his beliefs and lost everything save his integrity. The first item in his will points to his character and reflects his concern with settling a debt incurred nearly fifty years earlier.

> Whereas I am indebted to Messrs Ogleby and Faulkner, formerly of Pensacola in the sum of two hundred pounds upon a certain note of hand given by me to them several years since and I have been endevouring for a length of time to find out the parties in order to pay them, but have not as yet succeeded. I do hereby direct my Executors hereinafter named to advertise in the public prints for a term of one year after my decease for the said note of hand and if forthcoming within that period to pay the same out of my property.

Not mentioned in his will, in which he makes various bequests to nephews and others in England and to the couple who had looked after him in Halifax, was any reference to his son. This is almost certainly because he did not know he had a son.

Sehoy Taitt, the Creek girl whom David Taitt had married when he was Indian agent, bore him a son whom she named Davy. Davy Taitt grew up to become a friend of Aleck McGillivray son of Alexander McGillivray, the Creek leader whose Scottish father had a large estate in the Highlands. Aleck and Davy went to Scotland where they stayed at the McGillivray seventeen thousand acre ancestral home at Dunmaglass. They both went on to study at Banff, Scotland. Davy then went home to America to take advantage of a generous inheritance from his mother, Sehoy, for under Creek custom a man's property belongs to his relations on the maternal side. In 1809 Davy Tate, (note the change of spelling), was reported to be living well on the banks of the Alabama River.

Sehoy remarried after David had left. Her second marriage was to a Charles Weatherford. They had a son named William Weatherford who grew up to become the celebrated warrior, Red Eagle who fought against Andrew Jackson in the War of 1812.

All this would have been unknown to David Taitt. He died in Halifax and is buried in St. Paul's Churchyard where the stone reads, "Sacred to the Memory of David Taitt, Esq. A native of North Britain and a Captain in the late Indian Department who departed this life on 4th of August, 1834. Aged 94 years."

THE CANTANKEROUS MAYOR

David Mathews was a curiosity among politicians. Not only does it appear that few liked him but he generated controversy wherever he went – sometimes simply for the sake of it, possibly because he had no need of popular votes. It must surely be that there were people who liked him and with a few cronies supported his appointments to various powerful positions. But when he came as a Loyalist to Nova Scotia seeking further employment as a lawyer, the Halifax establishment was quick to send him packing down to Cape Breton as the first Attorney General there.

Mathews is remembered only by history buffs today as the man who, when mayor of New York, was involved in a plot to have George Washington assassinated or, as some thought, simply kidnapped. In Cape Breton he is remembered as the man who sought to destroy the career of our first Lieutenant Governor.

The days of the American Revolution were tumultuous. Family loyalties were ripped apart, an illustrative example being that of Benjamin Franklin, founding father of the new America, whose son William was a Loyalist. In this the Mathews' family were somewhat different – they were all Loyalists – and whatever else may be said of them, their allegiance was to their king, their country and themselves.

No doubts about loyalty troubled David Mathews. Graduate in law from Princeton College, New Jersey, Mathews was appointed Mayor of New York by the British Governor of the colony, William Tryon in February, 1776 after the resignation of the previous mayor, Whitehead Hicks. Four months later the city was rife with rumour and fear. Rebellion had begun and the rebel Continental Army, commanded by General George Washington, was stationed around the city. On the same day in June Washington rode into the city to be received by tumultuous crowds, Tryon was greeted only by Mayor Mathews, and some assemblymen and Anglican ministers. Both rebel and loyal forces tried to exercise authority but late that month British troops and Governor Tryon left what little security the city offered for a warship anchored in the habour. Days later Mathews was arrested.

A body with the ominous title of "The Committee for Detecting and Defeating Conspiracies" under the chairmanship of John Jay had conducted hearings since the previous month. Its first witnesses were prisoners from the city jail and it met at Scott's Tavern on Wall Street. A counterfeiter named Isaac Ketchum told the committee that two other prisoners, Michael Lynch and Thomas Hickey, facing the same charge had tried to recruit him for the British side. They had both decided to abandon the American cause and cast their lots in with the British. This was particularly worrying since Hickey was a member of Washington's prestigious bodyguard. Others were soon implicated and money, it was said, had been distributed to bend loyalties. The money had come from Governor Tryon with an additional hundred pounds contributed by Mayor Mathews.

Conspirators, some say as many as forty of them who had met at various taverns near Washington's headquarters, were quickly arrested. Mathews was not in the city but at his home at Flatbush in Brooklyn. On the night of 21 June Washington's men burst into his home. In his words, he was "dragged out of bed by an officer and twenty men of the rebel army" and was put into close confinement in the city jail. The city soon resonated with rumour. One report widely circulated was that Washington was to be poisoned and that chickens thrown peas from Washington's plate had promptly died. Another had it that the city powder magazine was to be blown up and the city handed back to the British in the confusion. Yet another was that Washington would be kidnapped when he visited his mistress. This last rumour was partially substantiated by Hickey's court marshal proceedings. One witness, James Clayford, admitted to being Mary Gibbons' lover and said that she was also Washington's mistress. Said Clayford, "The general maintained (her) very genteelly at a house near Mr. Skinner's... he often came there very late at night in disguise."

Hickey was found guilty on 27 June and sentenced to death. The following day at 10am in a field in the Bowery before thousands of spectators he was hanged. Wrote General Washington to his men,

> The unhappy Fate of Thomas Hickey, executed this day for Mutiny, Sedition and Treachery, the General hopes will be a warning to every soldier in the Army, to avoid those crimes And all others so disgraceful to the character of a Soldier, and pernicious to his country, whose pay he receives and whose Bread he eats. And in order to avoid those crimes the most certain method is to keep out of the temptation of them, and particularly to avoid lewd Women, who, by his dying

Confession this poor Criminal first led him into practices which ended in an untimely and ignominious Death.

David Mathews and others remained in the city jail while in and around New York a hunt for suspected Loyalists was pursued with vigour. According to Supreme Court Judge Thomas Jones – himself a Loyalist – they "were pursued like wolves and bears, from swamp to swamp, from one hill to another…in consequence… numbers were taken, some were wounded and a few murdered".

Mathews was not tried and evidence against him at that time appears scanty. At a hearing following Hickey's execution he argued that Governor Tryon had simply given him some money to be passed on to a gunsmith for some guns he made for the governor. Mathews was ordered to remain in jail pending trial but with the arrival of the British fleet in the harbour he was sent to Connecticut. He may have welcomed that as a reprieve from an expected fate. A letter in the archives of the New York Historical Society states, "A gentleman who has escaped from the Provincials at New York and joined the army under General Howe wrote to a correspondent in London, '… Governor Franklin, accompanied by that merryheart David Mathew, Mayor of New York, now under sentence of death for eminent proofs of Loyalty to his King and the old Constitution, are removed into the Connecticut government for the better security of their persons'."

Mathews was sent to Litchfield on 1 July on the same day that another memorable event occurred. The lead statue of George III, erected on Bowling Green in 1770, was torn down by an angry mob, cut into pieces and sent to Litchfield to be melted down and turned into ammunition. It seems likely that Mathews was a part of the same convoy. He was in the custody of a Captain Moses Seymour and was probably treated with some courtesy since on arrival he gave the captain the "pleasure carriage" in which he had traveled. A statistical account of the town of Litchfield in 1812 refers to the first "pleasure carriage" as a chair "brought into this town by Mr. Mathews, mayor of New York City, in the year 1776, and is still in use here."

According to the records of the Litchfield Historical Society Mathews, who was kept in jail on East Street was soon moved because he became "the storm center of many rumours" and his life was believed to be in imminent danger. His next stop was Hartford but the situation there was even worse. "...the Convention will not furnish me with some resolve of certificate to enable me to contradict a most hellish report that has been propagated, and is verily believed throughout the Colony that I was concerned in a Plot to assassinate General Washington and blow up the magazine in New York. The Convention know that (the report) is as false as hell is false." A few years later, in the safety of Nova Scotia and seeking compensation for his losses during the war, Mathews admitted to his involvement in the plot. In the meantime, Hartford did not want him and to avoid a possible lynching he was soon on his way back to Litchfield.

What happened next is far from clear. We know that after only a few days Mathews escaped from jail and was soon back in New York City that had now been recaptured by the British. According to Litchfield records he was permitted a degree of freedom. "He walked abroad for the benefit of the air (as he was permitted to do) and neglected to return – very much to the satisfaction of all concerned in his detention." The New York Tory papers had a different spin on his escape. He had "effected an escape an escape with great danger and difficulty" Years later, after the end of the war David Mathews made a claim to the Royal Commission on the Losses and Services of

American Loyalists for compensation for the 150 pounds sterling it had cost him – presumably in bribes – to make his escape. Arriving back in New York Governor Tryon made him a gift of 50 guineas.

Mathews soon took advantage of being restored to his various positions of authority. Information is scant but one source is from the writings of a Loyalist judge, Thomas Jones. Jones was well connected. He was married to Anne de Lancey, daughter of New York's Lieutenant Governor, James de Lancey, and following a distinguished legal career had been appointed to the New York Supreme Court 1773. He was one of the fifty-nine Loyalists, including Mathews, attainted by the state's Forfeiture Act – which meant that he lost his entire estate to the rebels and should he return to New York he would be hanged. He was arrested three times during the war and was twice taken as a prisoner to Connecticut. His health was severely damaged but he managed to get to England where he wrote a bitter attack upon the republicans and also on British officials in America whom he blamed for losing the war. Many years later his writings were published and he makes no effort to conceal his disdain for David Mathews.

On returning from Litchfield Mathews resumed his position as mayor and acting magistrate of the police court. "General Howe, with great generosity" wrote the sarcastic Jones, "made a present (of what was none of his own) of all the profits arising from the ferries, markets and slips to David Mathews, Esq, which he was pleased to accept of, and in violation of his oath…Not content with General Howe's gift the mayor ordered all the tenants of the Corporation to pay their rents to him, which he received without a blush, without shame, compunction or remorse and modestly appropriated the whole to his own use." Jones also tells us that Mathews, in addition to being thoroughly dishonest, was like most American mayors "a mere ignoramus in matters of law

…as any common packhorse in the country". "Mathews laid all the butchers in New York markets under contribution and compelled each to send him every day what provisions he wanted for himself and his family. They were obliged to comply and the Mayor was supplied with his provisions without any charge or expense."

In his final years in New York before appointment to the post of Attorney General of the Colony of Cape Breton, Mathews lived well. Jones, clearly not one to mince words, described him as "a person low in estimation as a lawyer, profligate, abandoned, and dissipated, indigent, extravagant and luxurious, head over heels in debt, with a large family as extravagant and voluptuous as himself and no method of supplying his wants until this "judicious" appointment (to the police court). After which, with the assistance of General Howe's present of the revenues of the City Corporation and by exercising every kind of villany, extortion, oppression, peculation and rapine upon a set of loyal subjects deprived of the benefits of law… he became before the end of the war a man of great property, lived in the style of a gentleman, gave what the military described as "dammed good dinners", wallowed in luxury, and rioted upon plunder illegally and unjustly extorted from His Majesty's loyal subjects within the lines, to whom on every occasion he behaved with all the haughty superciliousness of a Turkish Bashaw or a proud, overbearing Highland Scottish Laird".

Although the British were defeated in the American War of Independence, New York City remained in their hands until its final evacuation at the end of November, 1783. Prior to that date a number of associations were formed to process the evacuation of refugees, some twenty-nine thousand of them, to Quebec and Nova Scotia. Their prospects were bleak and those who were unemployed professionals faced a most uncertain future. Nova Scotia was soon stocked with what one of them described as "starved lawyers". The Governor of Nova Scotia, John Parr, was not sympathetic to them, possibly because many of these Loyalists wanted William Franklin to be appointed governor. Whether or not Parr knew of Mathews' reputation is not known but there was no job for him in Halifax. The only position available was in Sydney as Attorney General to the new colony of Cape Breton where the first Lieutenant Governor, Frederick DesBarres, had established his capital.

The population in and around Sydney in those early days was composed of Loyalists, most who had come from the American colonies via Quebec under the auspices of Abraham Cuyler, former mayor of Albany, New York, and DesBarres' English group who had crossed the Atlantic. In addition to settlers in the Sydney area there were Loyalist settlers at Baddeck and Acadians on Isle Madame. There were also Mi'kmaq Indians and a few independent Loyalist settlers, for example, those in the Port Hood area. The council for the new colony was also divided in its opinions and origins. A frequent source of dispute was the distribution of food supplies but acrimony extended into numerous other areas. An example is in the selection of wardens for Saint Georges Church whose priest was Anglican Ranna Cossit, a Loyalist from New Hampshire. David Mathews was proposed. His nomination was unanimously rejected.

Yet the first and perhaps the major confrontation between Loyalists and English concerned food. Food for the Loyalists and soldiers of the garrison was sent down from Halifax by the military there to Major Yorke, commanding the 33rd Regiment in Sydney. But the English settlers needed food as well and DesBarres tried to distribute some of the rations to the non-loyalist settlers and contended that, as

Lieutenant Governor food distribution for all settlers was his concern. Yorke objected; the supplies had been sent to him. Mathews and Cuyler supported Yorke in the dispute while most of the settlers appear to have supported DesBarres. The council was split with DesBarres finally buying supplies on his own account. Mathews, Cuyler and Yorke complained to London that DesBarres' conduct was "painful to British born subjects", curious but not inaccurate wording since both former mayors had been born in the American British colonies. Nevertheless, the complaint fell on receptive ears. DesBarres lost his job and was replaced by William Macarmick, from Truro in England.

Macarmick sought to strengthen the office of Lieutenant Governor, undermined in the disputes with DesBarres. He drove Cuyler from the colony and so weakened Loyalist influence. The battles continued between the factions in the council. The Reverend Cossit, as minister, was responsible for selecting the schoolteacher. Mathews and his followers refused to send their children to the school. But when Macarmick retired Mathews was senior councilor and he in turn threw Ranna Cossit off the council. He then appointed his son, David Mathews junior as acting attorney general, and another son, William Tryon Mathews provost marshal to replace another opponent, David Taitt. He imprisoned Ranna Cossit on debt charges and had the Chief Justice dismissed. The bickering between the two factions continued. In 1798 Mathews was himself ejected from the council by the incoming Lieutenant Governor. A few years later Anglican Bishop Inglis came down from Halifax to relieve Cape Breton of its controversial cleric. He feared that Cossit might lead the people into becoming "Methodists, Catholics or infidels" and transferred him to Yarmouth.

Prior to that, in July of 1800 David Mathews died. Cossit would not allow his body in the churchyard and it is believed that he was finally buried on his own property at Point Amelia, across the harbour from Sydney in what is now Petersfield Park. The career of a most cantankerous man had ended but he had established a pattern of dispute and acrimony that would last at least another generation.

BALL BROTHERS - PARADOXES IN AN AGE OF PARADOX

It was the social event of 1795. Ingram Ball's young wife Margaret was preparing for the baptism of her son at St Georges, the garrison church in Sydney. Reverend Ranna Cossit was to officiate and by good chance her brother-in-law Alexander Ball was in town. Husband Ingram, just two years in the colony was a member of the Cape Breton Council and also acting jointly in the office of Chief Justice. More auspicious than that, Lieutenant Governor Macarmack was to sponsor the child, along with Ingram's brother Alexander.

That Ingram and Margaret Ball had so rapidly become significant social figures was not surprising. He had, at his own expense, enlisted fifty young men, tenants on the family estate of Stonehouse in Gloucestershire, into the army to fight in the American War. He himself served initially as a captain Royal Dragoons and when war ended returned to the family estates. His brothers became prominent. Brother George was a major in the Royal Marines, brother Alexander, now in Sydney for the baptism, was a rising naval officer, and brother

Levi had developed business connections in India. There was also a sister, Henrietta Mary, but she appears to have been unmarried.

Ingram, now thirty-three years old and a widower, married nineteen-year old Margaret Childs, the daughter of a banker at St Marylebone Church in London. Stonehouse Court was sold. He received some of the proceeds and was perhaps attracted to Cape Breton by reports of brother Alexander. Alexander, as a lieutenant in the 14-gun sloop *Atalanta*, had patrolled the North American coast including Nova Scotia and Newfoundland. Now Ingram and his family headed for Cape Breton. They may also have been attracted by the promise of a grant of one thousand acres of land a few miles from town. The Balls were quickly prominent figures in Sydney's social hierarchy.

Despite the appearance of social harmony at the baptism there were constant strains on the equanimity. An unsigned letter from Cape Breton to London somewhat later implies that disorderly elements in town made life difficult. "I wish I could impress you with a just idea of the state of our Courts of Law" wrote an anonymous correspondent:

> Our acting Attorney General (young Mr. Mathews) associated with the Commander of a sloop of war …and others of their officers have for three weeks kept the town of Sidney(sic) in constant alarm, by their dissipation: rummaging almost every night, …. The houses of even respectable Inhabitants for Servant Maids and Women of suspected fame, whose haunts are discovered by the lawyer…and who a night or two ago broke into the house of Judge Ball, who being indisposed lay that night at his Office, to avoid the noise of children; seized Mrs. Ball, as discreet a person as any in the island, teized her and tossed her about for some time, whilst his partners

and a strumpet in their company were looking through the window delighted at the show; at length finding means by stiring(sic) the fire to produce a light, she recognized the Gentleman through his disguise, and he was glad to retreat. As she is not very inviting, no doubt it was meant as an insult on the unfortunate husband; who being now reduced to one third part of his former salary, by the appointment of two assistant judges….that I suppose he will not venture to show resentment, nor is it now well in his power, the Provost Marshall being brother-in-law to the Assailant….These gents are so regardless of character that, a few days ago, they made a trip up the river some miles for a strumpet, whom the Attorney General and the Captain had seated between them at noon-day and carried into town, in the face of the Inhabitants.

The behavior of David Mathews' son and his naval officer friends was not the only example of the behavior of senior people in the community, incomprehensible by today's standards, that illustrate the coarse standards of the age. George Moore, a naval officer and member of Macarmack's Council raped a fifteen-year old slave girl named Diana Bustian in government house and she had twins as a result. One of the twins was stillborn. Diana appealed to George Moore and his brother for assistance. None was given and Diana died shortly afterwards. These were probably regarded as honorable men and certainly the mere fact that those settlers who were Loyalists had surrendered everything they had except their principles would attest to this. Yet this rape appears to have occurred without social sanction against the rapist. Major John Murray of the garrison also fathered a child by a black woman and while this may or may not have been technical rape it is difficult to imagine it as less than gross exploitation.

The behavior of so many in and visiting Cape Breton reflects the social nature of the times back in England. In 1780 mobs participating in the so-called Gordon Riots burned to the ground parts of London. From the highest to the lowest wild behavior was almost endemic. Despite Jane Austin's novels of polite society in England's rural areas the towns could be a glaring contrast. From the antics of the Prince of Wales to the gin palaces portrayed earlier by Hogarth "the mob" was always feared. England at that time was a country of paradoxes and it is hardly surprising that some of the excesses were transferred to a remote colony, particularly since reports suggest that the principal retail trade of the colony was in rum.

We know that Ingram Ball was on social terms with Lieutenant Governor Macarmick by letters of the times. In the winter of 1794 he spent a day and night at the governor's house at York Fields (today's Petersfield). He asked the governor if he could borrow a small amount of hay for his own cow. The governor hesitated, "I really don't know how I can, " replied Macarmick, "for I am apprehensive from the report my people make that I shall run short of hay." Ball then said something to the effect that he only wanted a small amount, to which the governor made no answer except to wish him good night. Ball took some hay and had it sent to Sydney. Later, another guest at the governor's house, the sister of the Honourable James Miller, Superintendent of the Mines, said she heard Macarmick state that Ball had stolen his hay. Ball defended himself from this accusation by saying that the governor "has peculiar frailities of temper and he was at times extremely hasty."

Ball also remembered, in order to erode the reliability of Mrs. Miller's statement, the governor's complaints against the Millers, who had stayed at the Government House at Yorkfields for some time in 1794. When Ball and the governor were walking in the garden an immense cloud of feathers billowed from one of the windows. The governor rushed into the house, then returned and complained, "Could you believe it Ball, that Miss Miller would treat me in such a rude and disrespectful manner. She borrowed money from me yesterday to buy feathers from the Indians and she is now manufacturing them into beds in my rooms upstairs" Later the governor complained that the Miller's servant was stealing vegetables from his garden, "Observe that servant, Ball, what he is about. Could you believe that Mr. Miller, without ever asking my leave, has ordered his servant to strip my garden of its choicest vegetables. Surely no gentleman at home would act so by another. I really am at a loss to conceive what idea this man has brought to America, and where he was bred." Despite all this the Lieutenant Governor agreed to sponsor the Ball's son at the baptism.

Whether the irascible governor was at fault or the Millers or Ball is not now known, but on 26 May, as Macarmick was about to leave the island, he left a letter of commendation with Ball stating that he wished to testify "my high sense of the faithful manner in which you have executed the trust reposed in you as an Assistant Judge of the Supreme Court, and particularly so since you have acted singly on the bench"

Events that followed illustrate the ongoing tensions and the rapid decline and fall of the Ball's social prominence. .

With Macarmick gone Mathews became administrator and appointed Archibald Dodd, one of his allies, as a first assistant judge, which act apparently suspended Ball from the bench. Mathews also kicked him off the Council. Later Mathews used a debt charge as an excuse to jail Ball. In the summer of 1798 James Ogilvie arrived as Lieutenant Governor and released Ball and put him back on the Council, at the same time dismissing Dodd.

Soon Ball would not be "acting singly on the bench". He was joined by the Honourable William Smith and they shared the role. This was the beginning of further problems for Ball. Ball and Smith were soon constantly bickering. The next administrator, John Murray, called Ball "an old military debauchee" and accused him of being drunk "from Morning to night". Ball was soon in serious trouble. The problem was again money or, more precisely his indebtedness to merchants in Sydney. In the eighteenth century indebtedness was far more seriously regarded than now. In England thousands were clapped into prison because of their difficulty in paying off their debts. In the 1770s almost half the entire prison population of England were debtors. The conditions there were brutish and it was the creditor not the court that confined them. Ingram Ball fell foul of the system, in part because of his poor relationship with the William Smith with whom he now shared the bench.

In 1799 complaints were made against Ball to the other joint Chief Justice, Smith, by a William Baker who claimed that Ball had committed perjury by swearing that Baker owed him money. Joint Chief Justice Smith forwarded this complaint to London and Ball entered into a furious correspondence to protect his reputation. He did it by way of counter attack, "a most infamous character, a Mr. William Baker, a Ci-devant (formerly) bankrupt linen draper from Ludgate Hill. This man some four years ago (shocking to relate) had a child now living by his wife's sister, and they all reside under the same roof." General Murray, now the governor, apparently supported Mr. Smith and had Ball suspended from the council. A flurry of angry correspondence erupted between Sydney and the Office of the Secretary of State in

London. Ball apparently thought it relevant to report that Smith was so convinced that was to be the sole Chief Justice, rather than holding the post jointly with Ball, that he remarked that Smith "brought with him the scarlet robe and large wig appertaining to the office." But, Ball could not help adding, "they do not appear to have been made for him; and they are a good deal tarnished."

Apparently Baker's account book, which Smith saw, showed Ball to be much in debt to Baker. Ball claimed that Smith was ignorant of the amount that Baker owed him. Angry correspondence continued largely due, if one is to believe Ball's side of the story, to a misunderstanding of an action taken by Ingram's brother, Captain Alexander Ball. Captain Ball deposited a number of Bills guaranteeing sums of money payable to Ingram on the presentation of various bills. There was so much venom in the correspondence and irreconcilable division in the community, that at this late date it is impossible to unearth the truth of the matter. Even the Anglican Minister was drawn into the fray. Said Ball, 'it proves Mr. Cosset to be divested of every principle of Christianity."

In November, 1799 Ball wrote to the Secretary of State in London complaining of a conspiracy against him but he was removed from office in December. In the Spring of 1800 he was brought to trial. He was told that if he would confess to perjury and leave the island he would be released immediately and given money to see him on his way. He refused stating that not only would this be a stigma on his honour but would also reflect upon the honour of his brother, Captain Ball.

In the Spring of 1800 he was tried, found guilty and sentenced the be imprisoned for twelve months, fined twenty pounds sterling and ordered to leave the island for three years. He wrote to London outlining the services of himself and his family to the nation and explaining "I am with a wife and eight children mostly infants, left entirely destitute, in a country where there are no rich neighbours or friends to assist the poor and needy."

In early 1801 the new administrator, John Despard, started to write to London on Ball's behalf. In October 1801 Ball was still in jail and wrote to the Secretary of State in London that he had now been twenty two months in prison "Notwithstanding that His Majesty has been most graciously pleased to remit the whole of the iniquitous sentence passed against me....I am still in confinement to the great distress of myself, wife and numerous family. The two civil actions against me are uniquitous(sic) and unjust (one for 75 pounds and 5 shillings the other for 31 pounds,18shillings) both plaintiffs having absconded from this settlement a few months ago in the most shameful and unprincipled manner." Ball pleaded that in view of his having spent thirty years in the service of the crown and his brother Alexander having been so successful commanding *the Alexander* at the Battle of the Nile, some provision now be made for himself and family "now left entirely destitute".

At some point Ball was released – or the jailhouse conditions were far from stringent - for another child, Phoebe, was born in the Spring of 1802.

Brother Alexander after ending his visit to Sydney was, while Ingram struggled to overcome his various problems, literally sailing onto glory. Much earlier, two days after Ingram had married Margaret Child at St Marylebone Church in London on 5 July, 1785, Captain Alexander Ball also married, to a lady eleven years his senior, but curiously not at the same church, but at St James', Westminster. Five more years would pass before what must have seemed an interminable period of "leave on half pay", the plight of British naval officers in peacetime. But in the summer of 1790 he was given command of a frigate. Three years later, in command of a larger frigate, the *Cleopatra*, he was back patrolling the Newfoundland and Nova Scotian coast, enabling him to be at his nephew's baptism.

In 1797 Ball, now in command of the 74-gun *Alexander* joined Admiral Jervis' fleet off Cadiz, and under the orders of Captain Horatio Nelson, set off for Aboukir Bay, Egypt. It was just a few days later that Ball and the *Alexander* towed Nelson's storm-crippled ship into Sardinia, marking the beginning of a close friendship between Ball and Nelson. When Nelson, an emotional man, boarded Ball's ship he embraced him saying, "A friend in need is a friend indeed".

On 1 August, 1798, Nelson defeated Napoleon's fleet. The *Alexander* sustained seventy-two casualties in the battle, only two of them dead the others, including Ball, wounded. The battle over Nelson's words, as it was about to begin, had come true. "Before this time tomorrow I shall have gained a peerage, or Westminster Abbey". Napoleon's Asian and African ambitions were destroyed along with his fleet.

Ball was ordered to blockade the island of Malta, which dragged on over the next two years. He earned the affection of the islanders, who were in as dire circumstances as a result of occupation by the detested French garrison, by seizing a number of Neopolitan supply ships and handing all the food in them to the islanders. In 1801 Ball was created a baronet and Governor of Malta. Though he commanded no more ships he rose, by virtue of seniority to the rank of rear admiral. The people of Malta admired him and he them. Some of the English settlers there thought he favored them too much but Ball replied that he had won the island largely with the aid of the Maltese and that the British held it by their free-will, as fellow subjects and fellow-citizens.

It has been speculated that Ingram Ball lived beyond his means and owed merchants money. He was forced to mortgage land to pay off debts. It is also speculated that Alexander Ball advanced him a substantial amount of money for which Ingram gave him the deed of his property. He died 18 March, 1807, and was buried at St. George's Church. It is also speculated that although Ingram left his acres to his children they could not get clear title to it since it was actually owned by their uncle.

Early in his career Alexander had sailed around our coast, but later he was kept busy in the Mediterranean. Alexander Ball died in office on Malta in 1809, two years after his brother's death, and is buried on the island. Ingram had died two years earlier but Alexander remembered the children in his Will. He stated that Oak Farm was to be for the exclusive use of the children of Ingram Ball who might choose to reside on it.

CAPTAIN THOMAS CRAWLEY

The early council of the colony of Cape Breton was distinguished by constant acrimony. Squabbling factions led by Attorney General David Mathews and the Reverend Ranna Cossit must have caused despair in London and wonder if the Lieutenant Governors of the colony would ever preside over a smooth administration.

Yet one councilor emerged relatively unscathed from the bedlam of local government - Captain Thomas Crawley who was first appointed in 1789 at the age of thirty-two. An early mention concerned his volunteering to help organize an expedition to catch moose poachers. When the Council passed an ordinance controlling the slaughter of moose and caribou it was hoped that the poachers would be caught. They were not but Crawley had made his early appearance on the pages of Cape Breton Council history in a manner unlikely to earn the ire of other members. That itself was something of a distinction.

Crawley was born in 1759 in Ipswich in eastern England. He joined the Royal Navy and during the American Revolution served under Admiral Sir Peter Parker on *HMS Bristol*. Parker, an irascible and cantankerous officer, made a disastrous showing at the Battle of

Sullivan's Island, off Charleston, which he lost through relying on local pilots. Some of his fleet ran aground and the *Bristol* came under heavy shore fire. Among his lieutenants were Thomas Crawley and Horatio Nelson, neither of whom was numbered among the many casualties. Parker, whose britches were blown off by one shot, despite being the victim of humorous satire in England, soon rose to be Admiral of the Fleet.

The *Bristol* sailed north for New York and it may have been there that Crawley met with other Loyalists and, because of his association with them, eventually decided to join those who came a few years later to Cape Breton. Whatever the reason, he first went to England where he married an Esther Bernal, the daughter of a wealthy Jewish family that had converted to Christianity, and brought her to the island with him. Later the couple and their family became prominent in the growth of the Baptist Church in Sydney.

The Crawleys purchased land adjacent to David Mathews on the Westmount side of the harbour. Later they acquired the Mathews' property and the so-called Mathews' Creek became Crawley's Creek. The area is now Petersfield Provincial Park.

In 1805 Crawley, a man of many talents, was appointed Surveyor-General. Over the three decades Crawley was involved in portioning out land grants to new immigrants. After the arrival of the Loyalists and English settlers in 1785, another body of immigrants arrived from St. Pierre following the outbreak of the French Revolution. Early in the nineteenth century the first wave of Scots landed. Accompanied by Captain William Cox, after whom Coxheath is named, and guided by Mi'kmaq guides, Crawley laid out the base lines for surveys and planned the land grants across the island. According to Dr. Robert Morgan the Acadians from St. Pierre generally wanted small plots along the water's edge so that they could continue fishing, while the Scots wanted two hundred acre grants.

The Scots came in their thousands in the first quarter of the nineteenth century. By 1815 the population was estimated to be 6,000 and by 1827 it had reached 18,700. Ten years later the population had climbed to 35,420. Crawley's task was enormous. In addition he was concerned at the theft of coal by smugglers. In 1820 Crawley reported that in that year alone eleven smugglers from Main a Dieu and Sydney had stolen a thousand chaldrons of coal - a chaldron was a volume equal to thirty-six bushels. This coal was usually sold in Halifax, where demand often exceeded supply or, after regulations had been tightened, at some of the numerous outports. At much the same time, but beyond the control of Crawley, American ships were stealing large quantities of gypsum from near the Strait of Canso.

In 1817, during the Lieutenant-Governorship of General Ainslee, argument between councilors and Ainslee matched in bitterness those of the earliest administration. Between 1817 and 1818 two councilors, Bruce and Dumaresq, were replaced by two military officers and the Judge of Probate dismissed – although this order was immediately countermanded by Lord Bathurst. Ranna Cossit (junior) was suspended from his office of Comptroller of Customs – he had neglected to collect the duty on rum – and the barrister at the Court of Chancery was forbidden to practice there.

In a letter to the Under Secretary of State in London, Ainslee denounced the inhabitants of the island generally as a set of deceitful unprincipled aliens, "embued with the Yankee qualities of the refuse of three kingdoms". Ainslee also blamed the London Ministry for what he called their vacillating policy regarding land grants. Because of it many valuable settlers had left the island for the United States.

In London the government of Cape Breton must have appeared chaotic. The Colonial Secretary instructed Sir James Kempt, who was about to sail to Halifax to take over the government of Nova Scotia to annex Cape Breton to the mainland immediately upon his arrival. He reached Halifax 1 June and promptly informed General Ainslee of his intention to annex the island. General Ainslee left Sydney on 24 June on the brig *Hannah*, sailing direct to London. The Cape Breton Council met for the last time, appointing the senior military officer, a Captain David Stewart, to take over the administration until arrangements for the annexation were complete. At that final meeting the Councilors present, in addition to Captain Stewart, were the President, Archibald Dodd, David Taitt, Joshua Weeks, Charles Ward, Frederick Imthurn and Thomas Crawley.

The new government in Halifax promptly dismissed every office holder except Crawley. He and his knowledge were far too important to be abandoned for they could not be replaced. He knew the island better than anyone. Halifax knew little of the geography of the island or of its inhabitants. Crawley could tell the new government what the products of the island were and where they came from. Halifax was determined to lay out reservations for the Indians and Crawley surveyed them at Whycocomagh (Waycobah), Middle River (Wagmatcook) and Eskasoni. In later years Crawley played an indispensable role in obtaining assistance for islanders during the great famine of 1845-51 when successive crops of potatoes failed – matching a similar famine in Scotland and the notorious one in Ireland. Even after his death the Crawley name remained prominent in Nova Scotian history. One son became Commissioner of Crown Lands for Cape Breton, another founded the Arts Department at Acadia University and a third founded Horton Academy and became the first President of Acadia University.

JOHN AND MARY LEITCH – PRESS-GANGED AND SHIP-WRECKED

John Leitch, a respectable family man, living with his wife Nancy in Ayrshire Scotland was a weaver when the American Revolutionary War began. Just how he became embroiled in those events is not clear but there are significant clues.

Weaving in the lowlands of Scotland was expanding rapidly, becoming centralized south of Ayrshire in the city of Glasgow and there were frequent industrial disputes. Weavers had a seven-year apprenticeship and, married with children, unlikely to take to the streets in violent disputes – those came later.

When war in America began, recruiting for the army was more urgent. Having soldiers volunteer "to take the King's shilling" was always difficult. Because of the well-known savage discipline with its frequent floggings, poor pay and extended overseas service only the most desperate of men would volunteer. The navy had its own methods. Armed thugs roamed the streets of seaport cities and simply kidnapped men to serve at sea.

The army, always short of men, recruited mercenaries from across Europe, largely Hessians and Hanoverians contracted by their rulers to the British authorities. But that was hardly enough. During the American war recruiting acts were passed in 1777 and 1778 that allowed press gangs to "arrest" men simply for being drunk and disorderly and force them into the army. Some men it was said were so desperate that they cut off their own thumbs and forefingers to avoid being "pressed". Regimental colonels, responsible for raising numbers for their own regiments, may well have had many more than the "drunk and disorderly" swept up in the net cast by press gangs. It is possible, though there is no way now of knowing for certain, that John Leitch working in Glasgow or visiting was simply grabbed with other unfortunates and "pressed" into the army. Soon he was on his way to North America.

Nancy, back in Ayrshire, struggled on to raise her family with little idea until later of where John was.

How John found his way into the Royal Carolina Regiment is not now known. It is possible, however, that after his detachment of soldiers arrived in New York they were transferred to the regiment of Colonel Archibald Campbell – also from Ayrshire – who received orders to take three thousand men from New York to invade Georgia. They captured Savannah in December then took Augusta. After this Colonel Campbell left for Savannah and home leaving Major John Hamilton in command. It is possible that at this time Leitch was transferred to the Royal Carolina Regiment.

The North Carolinas were soon under the command of General Cornwallis and along with all British troops surrendered at Yorktown. After this defeat many of the North Carolinas returned to Charleston and later continued onto St Augustine, Florida. From there the commander, Major Hamilton, mailed British military authorities (PRO 30/55/7653) requesting permission to leave Florida for a British Province.. In November 1783 they arrived at Country Harbour, Nova Scotia, where the regiment was disbanded.

And what of Nancy? She is still in Ayrshire with her growing family.

For reasons now unknown John Leitch, now a free man headed to Cape Breton in company with a Robert Hill and Colin Campbell and received land at Schooner Pond near what is now Glace Bay. Unhappy with their location Hill and Cambell relocated to the Northwest Arm. Leitch it was said was lonely and in constant fear of bears that had tried to force their way into his log cabin. He set out one day in 1789 from what is now Meloney's Creek and eventually came to a rise of land overlooking Little Bras d'Or. He stayed there for some time with a friendly family but finally with difficulty persuaded the Lieutenant Governor to change his original lease. A surveyor drew the first line from the shore of the Bras d'Or parallel with what is now the Johnston Road and on 2 October, 1795, John Leitch received a crown grant of one hundred and fifty acres.

But how to get his wife over from Scotland? Many of the family were by then grown up, married and unwilling to leave but Nancy wrote that she would come just as soon as she could find a passage. It took more than two years but finally she found a vessel, an armed passenger ship, and headed out on the long voyage to Nova Scotia. The journey must have been appalling. Most of the immigrant ships at that time gave their passengers little more room than they would have had in a coffin, usually seventy-two by twenty-two inches. Berths were set so close on top that there was barely room to sit up. The food taken on at the beginning of the voyage would soon have deteriorated, the bread maggot- ridden, the meat full of weevils. Had the voyage taken longer than anticipated – and many did, some taking months – passengers could suffer from scurvy and dysentery as well as starvation. The voyage of Nancy Leitch appears to have been even worse than many others.

Britain was at war again with France. The United States was neutral and French warships and privateers hunted the North Atlantic for British ships heading to Canada and raiding coastal settlements, particularly drawn by the coal on Cape Breton's coast – little more than a decade earlier a major battle was fought off Sydney Harbour. Only the year before Nancy's journey hundreds of muskets were sent from Halifax for David Mathews, the attorney-general, to distribute to the Sydney militia, along with four-pounder cannons to Fort Dundas at Sydney Mines. A French squadron of nine ships was ordered to burn down Sydney but the gales of Fall drove them off. During Nancy's voyage a French warship attacked her ship. It was driven off though many passengers and crew were killed and the women passengers had to help carry the gunpowder and ammunition. The ferocity of the exploding cannons had been so great that Nancy Leitch suffered from deafness for the rest of her life.

Then her ship became a victim of the notorious dune-covered, windswept and desolate Sable Island, two hundred miles east of Halifax and known as the graveyard of the Atlantic. Sheer good fortune intervened. In 1798 the governor of Nova Scotia sent a schooner to the island to pick up castaways and Nancy and the other survivors were taken to Halifax and the mainland.

John Leitch, by this time had probably given up hope of ever seeing his family again. He was digging potatoes in his garden when he saw a friend, John Moffat hurrying towards him. He had news. Nancy

Leitch had just arrived from Halifax on the schooner *"Susan"*. Twenty years had passed since he had last seen her.

Little more is known of John and Nancy Leitch but it is possible that their last years were happy ones. One of their daughters, Margaret, had married a Robert Gammell in Glasgow in 1803. They came to Cape Breton in 1808. Initially settling on the north side of Indian Brook in Victoria County, Robert Gammell was later granted 168 acres at Little Bras d'Or near his wife's parents. He was successful. More important, the Gammells had five children, the first named John Leitch Gammell, so that in their remaining years John and Nancy Leitch had grandchildren to happily worry about while theirs and the land around them came to be called, as it is today, Leitch's Creek.

THANKFULL AND MARY – THE COSSITS AND MCLEODS

Two women, both with husbands well known in local history, both from utterly different backgrounds, both early settlers on Cape Breton, both of whose husbands seethed with passionate intensity, illustrate the tribulations suffered by many of their anonymous sisters in the early years of this island. They were Thankfull Cossit who came here in 1788 and Mary McLeod who came in 1820. Their husbands made an indelible stamp on the history of the island while they, perhaps bearing the weight of even greater anxiety, remain little known.

Thankfull Cossit must at some stage in her life reflected on the irony of her Christian name. How she viewed her life at the time cannot now be known but later viewers must have felt she had little to be thankful for.

Her husband, Ranna Cossit was born in Connecticut in 1744, studied at Rhode Island College and then, having decided he wanted to enter the Anglican Church, moved to England. In 1773 he was ordained and appointed a missionary of the Society For the Propagation of the Gospel in the Parish of Claremont, a wilderness community in New Hampshire that had been first settled only a dozen years earlier.

Even there the clouds of revolution were forming, although less rapidly than further south. But despite the unsettled times thirty-year-old Ranna Cossit met and married eighteen-year-old Thankfull Brooks. This teenage girl could hardly have guessed the hardships in store for her. Malicious mobs soon threatened her husband since Anglicans generally throughout the colonies believed in loyalty to the crown. Brought before the colonists' Committee of Safety, along with about twenty other Anglican priests of the colony, Cossit did nothing to disguise his loyalty and defiantly proclaimed his belief that the Tories would win. He was confined to the town with his wife and their first son.

Gradually the persecuted Loyalists left New Hampshire but Ranna Cossit stayed stubbornly on refusing to be cowed by his interrogators and even traveling north into Quebec in 1782 to give the authorities there information about the progress of the revolution in his area. Thankfull stayed behind. The war ended in 1783 but even then Cossit stayed on in the belief that New Hampshire and Vermont might return to the British flag. However, the Society for the Propagation of the Gospel was no longer allowed to employ missionaries in the United States and so Cossit had to find new employment that would provide income for himself and the ever-growing family.

Thankfull had not been idle in the interim. She had her first child, Ranna, a son, 1775, another, George Germain in 1777. The choice of the name was not arbitrary. Lord George Germain was then Colonial Secretary and exercised a decisive influence over military affairs in North America. By so naming their child at the height of the war, the Cossits were clearly and contemptuously cocking a snook at the "patriots" all around them. In 1779 they had a daughter Sophie, then another boy, Benjamin in 1780, a daughter, Phoebe in 1781 and then in 1784 another son, William, but he died two months later. However, in April 1785 she had another child Clementine. A couple of weeks after this birth Ranna received an offer of employment in the new colony of Cape Breton with a salary of 120 pounds a year, a house, glebe land and financial help in moving. He was also granted one thousand acres on the road to Louisbourg. It must have seemed as something approaching a miracle. Ranna sailed north, leaving his wife behind in Claremont with the children, to find out something of this new colony. Life in Claremont would not have been easy because of intense antipathy towards Loyalists.

Ranna had been promised both a church and a schoolhouse in Sydney so went back to Boston to gather supplies. He returned to Sydney again in 1786, once more leaving his wife behind with family now totaling six children, all under the age of eleven, until he could prepare a home for her. More setbacks; the temporary church and school had blown down in a gale, construction on his home had not begun and the government would not supply money for the new church until it was complete. Building the home, a substantial one with a number of fireplaces and initial work on the new church kept Cossit fully occupied and he was only able to return to the United States to his wife and children in the Fall of 1788. Thankfull may have been thankful for this absence. Although she became promptly pregnant again Ranna's absence meant an almost three year gap until the next birth.

In the spring of 1789 Ranna returned to Sydney with his family. Thirty-two-year old Thankfull and her six children settled into their new home on Charlotte Street. It still stands, an historic Loyalist home open to the public in the summer and fall. By the time she arrived, the community was already split and, as wife of a prominent citizen who loomed large in the disputes, would have been aware of enemies implacably opposed to her husband. Not a warm atmosphere for a new arrival, especially since she had just left a climate where she was a Loyalist and hence viewed by many as a traitor, and she was probably hoping for a better social environment.

Thankfull may have become accustomed to the disputes of her husband for she had stood by him during the bitter years of the American Revolution. She might reasonably have hoped that those acrimonious years were behind her. They were not. Soon her husband, now a member of the Council, was feuding with others – principally David Mathews – in a succession of disputes which tore apart any unanimity the little colony may have felt. Ranna tried to avoid some of these disputes, writing in 1786, before Thankfull arrived, "Seeing I could do no good in these matters I avoided as much as I conveniently could, anything, as I am determined, as much as in me lieth, to live peaceably with all men…"

Yet like Norman McLeod forty years on, Ranna Cossit held determined views and since, as an Anglican minister, he held that a duty of his church was to support the laws and precedents of the British constitution, he was soon embroiled. This involvement did not always sit favorably with the lieutenant-governors of the colony. He also traveled considerably visiting distant settlements at Main a Dieu, Louisbourg and Cow Bay (Port Morien). Later he taught school here and despite his constant battles with Mathews he appears to have loved life on Cape Breton. Thankfull's views we do not know. Money was always short and the demands of a growing family a constant source of anxiety. Even in an age of large families theirs was remarkable. Since coming to Sydney she had delivered Mary in 1789, John in 1791, a stillborn child in 1793, Thankfull Maxmilia in 1794 and Francis in 1797.

A garden was a necessity. Not only did she grow for her family to ensure that despite its size they would fed, but she also sold potatoes and mussels gathered on the shore to supplement her husband's income. Thankfull would have been familiar with a wide variety of vegetables. Many of those that grew in New England could be grown here and the seed was available. They ranged from beans, peas, cabbage and squash to the root vegetables such as beets, carrots, turnips, onions and, of course, potatoes. There was also a wide range of herbs both cultivated and wild for eating and medicinal purposes. As well in season there were wild strawberries, raspberries, blackberries, blueberries and apples.

But constant pregnancy and the disputaceous climate that surrounded her and her family must have sapped her health. 1802, five years after her previous pregnancy and at the age of forty-six, she died giving birth to her thirteenth child who was stillborn. Her husband's sad entry in the parish record suggests his grief. "… her whole life was ornamental to Christianity as a Wife, a Parent, a Neighboor…"

In 1805 Bishop Charles Inglis arrived in Sydney and persuaded Cossit that his long-standing political disputes in the community had caused scandal that could lead colonists into becoming "Methodists, Catholic or infidels". Cossit was appointed to the new parish of Yarmouth. He no longer involved himself in politics and died there in 1815.

At much the same time thousands of miles to the east a young woman anticipated marriage to a clergyman. Mary McLeod waited for the day when her espoused, Norman would complete his education and be able to marry her. Both Mary and Norman lived in Assynt, in Sutherland, northern Scotland. Thinly populated, many of the inhabitants lived close to the shore for the interior is mainly wild and desolate moorland. At the beginning of the century the many crofters occupied virtually every cultivatable spot, but after 1811 thousands were evicted from their homes in the interior by the Countess of Sutherland and her husband, Lord Stafford. The Duchess and her husband were keen to improve the land and to do that drove the inhabitants to the coast. Whether the two McLeods were a part of this clearance is not now known. But the whole of Britain at that time underwent a savage transformation as a result of industrialization and war. Unlike Thankfull Cossit, who spent her teenage years in an actual war zone, Mary McLeod, in the years after the great Napoleonic wars ended, must have seen many of its consequences.

"Next to a battle lost" famously lamented the Duke of Wellington as he surveyed the carnage of Waterloo, "the greatest misery is a battle gained." And the peace gained by the defeat of Napoleon, while better for the world than would have been his victory, brought great misery to the ordinary people of England and Scotland, a misery which had a profound impact on the development of Cape Breton by prompting emigration from Scotland to Nova Scotia.

The entire economy had for twenty years been directed to defeating the dictator of Europe. The end of the war brought a collapse of that economy.

Conditions were deplorable. All across the Highlands and Islands Scots were driven off their ancestral lands by poverty and the reforming zeal of landlords. A few years earlier a missionary to the Hebridean islands had described a *scallag*, "as a poor being who for mere subsistence becomes a predial slave to another, whether a sub-tenant, a tacksman or a laird. (He) builds his own hut, with sods and boughs of trees… five days a week he works for his master, the sixth he is allowed to himself for the cultivation of some scrap of land on the edge of some moss or moor on which he raises a little kail or coleworts, barley and potatoes…The only bread he tastes is a cake made of flour or barley." The Parliamentary Select Committee on Emigration, 1827-27 heard that on North and South Uist a third of the population was landless and entirely dependent on the charity of the local laird, MacDonald of Clanranald. Even before the Napoleonic War ended, the earlier breakup of the clan system and the need of tenants to make way for sheep had dire consequences in northern Scotland where, in a decade, as many as ten thousand had been driven from their land by the Countess of Sutherland, her husband and their agent. They actually paid people to clear out to Canada. In three years, one thousand people left northwest Sutherland alone for Upper Canada and Cape Breton.

The biographer of Norman McLeod does not touch upon these Clearances and their consequences and so it may be that they escaped much of the hardship. Certainly the Clearances gained momentum after the McLeods left and it is reasonable to speculate that the abandonment of allegiance to the established Church of Scotland by many Highlanders in favour of the Free Church in the first few decades of the century was another symptom of the general dissatisfaction.

In the towns of England riots were brutally suppressed. In Scotland rural dwelling crofters moved to the fishing villages or the cities or across the sea. Soon the McLeods were part of that exodus.

Norman McLeod was not an impoverished crofter (a tenant farmer on a small patch of land) but an educated man. Intent on entering the church he graduated from King's College, Aberdeen and then went to the University of Edinburgh to complete his studies for the ministry. Strongly opposed to the patronage and lax living of the established Church of Scotland, he soon broke with them and quit Edinburgh University before completing these studies. Returning to northwest Scotland, where Mary was patiently waiting for him, he taught school in Ullapool in the county of Ross and Cromarty and, when the resident minister was away, read the Scriptures and, most significantly, commented upon them. Though not a licensed preacher of the Church of Scotland, he soon had a popular following that, along with his anti-establishment theology, brought him into conflict with the minister. As a result he lost his job and to support his family – he had now married Mary and they had three sons, John Grant, Donald and Bunyan just born when father left for America – took to fishing.

Like many other Scots at that time he soon actively considered emigration and sailed from Ullapool for Nova Scotia. Mary's health had deteriorated, probably a result of constant worry and uncertainty, the birth of two children in rapid succession and the harsh conditions of life so she and the children would wait to follow him the next year.

Initially Norman settled in Pictou, a flourishing community grown prosperous in the timber trade, but after his family joined him he became disenchanted with prospects there and also perhaps by the community's excessive drinking, a result of vast quantities of rum from the West Indies trade. Mary now had a fourth child, a daughter Mary. Again, his preaching brought him a large following, known as "Normanites". Norman soon looked further westward, to Ohio. He and his followers built a boat, dubbed "the Ark" and set off, or so legend has it, to sail down the Atlantic coast to the Gulf of Mexico, then up the Mississippi to their destination. But to gradually hone their skills aboard their new boat they would first sail up the Northumberland Straits then around the top of Cape Breton into the Atlantic. This they did and soon after rounding Cape North sailed into St. Ann's Bay. There was no need to travel further. They had found what they wanted nearer to home than they had imagined and the following year Norman and his followers settled on the Bay.

Faithful Mary now had to adjust to a frontier life away from the sins but also from the conviviality of Pictou. In this new life trees had to be cut to build cabins, potatoes planted between the stumps, firewood, green, had to be cut and stored. Unlike Thankfull she came as part of a community. Thankfull lived in the town close to others, although many may have been hostile, but away from the support of old friends. But Mary lived in the forest and had to travel to friends, whose homesteads at St. Ann's were widely spaced and initially had little but trees between them. It was not until later that factions developed. In St. Ann's Alexander, the fifth child, was born, then came Murdock, Samuel, and Edward. A year later Margaret was born but soon afterwards little Edward died. The next year, when she was forty-three years old she had her tenth child, named, as was the custom after the Edward who had died.

James Duffus, on an island near Baddeck, kept the nearest store, but initially there were no established trails to it through the woods. Used to living either in the bare uplands of Assynt or among many Scots in Ullapool or in Pictou, the silent forest of Cape Breton may have been frightening and must have been daunting. Their own St Ann's Harbour was frozen over all winter and meals consisted largely of boiled potatoes and fish. Norman had his Calvinistic zeal to sustain him and the admiration of his followers to encourage him. Mary had more mundane concerns and worries.

Shortly after arriving at St. Ann's Norman was appointed magistrate and could perform marriages but, believing in the necessity of a religious service, he set off for the United States determined to be ordained as a minister. He was gone for a year leaving Mary to cope with all the essential chores and with raising the children, but returned as a licensed Presbyterian minister with all the powers, social and religious of that position. Interestingly, Norman McLeod had to go to the United States to be ordained while Ranna Cossit had had to leave America to go to England for his ordination.

Norman, never a man to keep his views to himself, particularly when expounding them from the pulpit of their little church, took to task any he assumed to have erred and even criticized Mary's bonnet during one sermon. He did not want her to set a precedent that might encourage younger and flightier women and he forbad women to wear ribbons or any such finery. When he became convinced that a young boy had committed a theft he ordered that a portion of the boy's ear be cut off. Such was his authority in their small community that the sentence was carried out. However, later it was found that another had committed the theft and some began to doubt Norman's infallibility and question his autocratic rule.

Mary's health may have been fragile. There are a number of references to this in Norman's biography. He refers to her as "a delicate spouse". And he mentions in his letters that she had "half dreaming notions of venturing along with me to Pictou to see several of her friendly acquaintances…". The poor woman may have been delicate but one must question this for how could a delicate woman survive the hardships of pioneer life. But she was probably also desperately lonely and, like most women of that time, unable to express herself.

Even when the community had developed nature stepped in to create new anxiety.

The western world now remembers the Irish potato famine but may be little aware how widespread that famine was in the 1840s. From Scotland to Newfoundland communities that relied heavily on the potato as their major source of food suffered from the results of potato blight. Cape Breton was no exception. In 1846, for example, the plight of residents of Inverness County was raised in the House of Assembly in Halifax. The potato crop in the county had suffered blight the previous summer. William McKeen of Mabou reported that half the crop had been lost and that which was saved might not keep through the winter. The people of South Lake Ainslee only had enough potatoes for two months and it was estimated that those in Skye Glen would have no food at all come St. Patrick's Day. The enormity of the problem was compounded by the need of people to eat potatoes stored for seed thus transforming a calamity into a long-term disaster.

Perhaps it was fear that the potato crop would fail and that famine would destroy his community, or perhaps a fear that his authority was eroding that prompted Norman to look further afield. Perhaps also it was his insatiable restlessness. Whatever the goad Norman's eyes now turned towards Australia. He had heard from his son who, after a long absence had written from Australia extolling its attractions and the mildness of the weather. Norman's thoughts focused on this new challenge, a journey of some twelve thousand miles. Maybe it was the ice in the harbour or the general exhaustion of winter, perhaps the bickering that had developed over the years, but soon many debated the possibility of mass exodus. Such was his influence that he persuaded eight hundred of the community to go to Australia with him. The first ship was built in the bay and set off for Australia in 1851.

They found this new country to be like Pictou only worse. Lawlessness was rife and typhoid fever broke out shortly after their arrival. Within weeks the three youngest children, Alexander, Samuel and Edward, who was now twenty-two, died. Disillusioned with Australia, Norman and his followers moved on to New Zealand where once again he was the dominant religious personality.

Mary stayed faithfully at his side but died three years after arriving in New Zealand, worn out by work and anxiety. Norman McLeod lasted into his eighty-sixth year sustained in part by his passionate intensity. It is reported that when he died a man who had not been on friendly terms with Norman offered to help one of the pallbearers. The bearer snapped at the volunteer, "Do you think I would let you touch his coffin?" The volunteer turned away, "All right", he said, "You can take him to hell yourself".

MURDER AND THE WASHED UP SAILORS

Many sailing ships foundered off the Cape Breton coast in the nineteenth century, but none with a more dire consequence to its survivors than one that ran aground on Petries Ledge in 1832.

Two of the survivors, Englishmen named Reuben Easman and William Johnston, walked to a tavern near where the North Sydney yacht club stands today, and asked the owners, a married couple named John and Charlotte Flahaven for shelter. Normally the Flahaven tavern was a simple eating and drinking establishment but the two Englishmen persuaded the Flahavens to let them board there, presumably until they could sign on to another ship.

The Flahavens had three daughters, one married named Ellen Linet and two unmarried girls, Catherine and Caroline, and a son Edward. Mrs. Flahaven was, to use today's jargon, "known to the police"– that is, she had done time. A dozen years earlier she had pleaded "not guilty" to theft but was found guilty. She was sentenced to three months in the Sydney jail. It would have been longer but she pleaded "benefit of clergy" and it was granted. This was a contrivance, dating from early medieval years when clergy had their own courts and were generally the only people who could read and write. This artifice had long since strayed from its original intent. In 1818 Mrs. Flahaven was able to recite the "Neck Verse" (of the fifty first psalm) so it could be formally said, "Legit ut clericus" or "she reads like a clerk" and her neck would be spared. Later, for lesser offenses, she could be spared a more draconian punishment. Unfortunately for her, by the time she really needed it, Benefit of Clergy had been totally abolished.

The Flahaven tavern was small. Upstairs was one large room. In it slept Mr. and Mrs Flahaven, their daughters Catherine and Caroline and their son Edward. Downstairs, adjacent to the tavern, was a small room where married daughter Ellen Linnet slept. The upstairs sleeping area had no partitions, not even a blanket dividing the beds. It was not long before, in the words of a witness that "an improper intimacy began" between Mrs. Flahaven and William Johnston. Mr. Flahaven objected to this but ineffectively since his wife continued to share Johnston's bed. At the later trial there was some suggestion that the other English sailor, Easman, was "in love" with one of the daughters, but this was not further pursued in court.

Tensions in the household mounted. John Flahaven tried to persuade the Englishmen to leave but when he overheard Johnston shout "If I had a pitchfork I'd run it though you" he became afraid for his life. There was some respite. Mrs. Flahaven and Johnston briefly left the house to stay with a neighbor but when they returned John became really frightened, went to the local magistrate, told him that his wife and her lover were bent on murder and that he needed protection. His plea was ignored.

Matters became worse. Mrs. Flahaven openly goaded her husband and Ellen Linnet overheard her mother say to Easman, "Remember what I told you. If you fail, never look me in the face again." Ellen, thinking this an idle threat, did nothing. John, in an effort to keep Johnston out, bolted the doors, but his wife sent one of the children to open a window so that Johnston could climb in when, in the words of a witness "He repaired to her bed, where he remained."

The following morning, 16 October, the two Englishmen untied a cow that had earlier been brought to the tavern for butchering. The cow, as they expected, took off for home along a track towards Little Bras D'Or. They then told John Flahaven that the cow, which was being fattened for the winter's meat, had escaped. Flahaven took off in hot pursuit, closely followed by the two sailors. They caught up with him and beat him to death one using a club, the other an axe.

Back home Ellen had seen them release the cow and follow her father. She then saw them return, spattered with blood. When Ellen asked where her father was Easman replied, "I've fixed him".

Johnson then became very much the head of the house and even ordered Ellen to wash his feet, which she refused to do. Ellen told one of her sisters, possibly the one that was alleged to be Easman's girlfriend, that she feared her father had been murdered. The sister passed this on to her mother, which provoked another rage. Said mother, "I'll wash my hands in Ellen's heart's blood for saying such a thing". Later that night Ellen overheard a conversation between her mother and the two sailors in which one of them told her, "He'll trouble you no more". They then began to fear that Ellen had overheard them and checked her room. But she had taken off heading for her uncle's home nearby. They almost caught up with her but when they saw she had reached safety returned to the tavern and, knowing the authorities would soon be after them, barricaded themselves in.

Ellen and her uncle headed to Leitches Creek and the Justice of the Peace who authorized three men to go to the tavern and arrest the sailors and Mrs. Flahaven. When they got there the building was too well fortified for them and more men had to be deputized before they could overcome the sailors and Mrs. Flahaven. Shortly after this, another party aided by John Flahaven's dog, found his partly buried body. His skull had been smashed, his throat cut and there were several other wounds.

The Supreme Court of Nova Scotia, sitting in Sydney on 27 August, 1833, almost a year after the crime, heard the trial. It was presided over by Judges Uniake and Hill. It was concluded the following day. Easman stated that he had gone with John Flahaven to help him find the cow but when Flahaven threatened him with a pistol there had been a struggle. He had hit Flahaven in self-defense and had accidentally killed him. He later retracted the statement saying that he had confessed because, for some reason, he was "in dread of the other two".

Charlotte Flahaven put all the blame on Easman. She and her lover, she said, were back at the house when Easman came back after chasing the cow and told her that he had killed her husband. Johnston corroborated her story saying that the murder was all Easman's fault.

The jury would have none of it. They were all three found guilty and sentenced to hang. Therein lay a problem. No one wanted to be hangman because of the fear that friends of the condemned might have their revenge later. Fortunately for the Sheriff an immigrant ship had docked the day before and yet another sailor was found to hang the threesome. The fee was five pounds but the sailor had to be locked in the jail so that he would not take off with the money before earning it.

On the morning of 19 September a militia guard was formed around the scaffold on Charlotte Street. Hundreds of spectators poured into town to witness the event and interest was intense, as it always had been in other parts of Canada when a woman was to be executed. The prisoners were said to have been quite calm although Mrs. Flahaven, on being told that her daughter Ellen was not there, replied that she wanted to see her so that she could kill her. She would do it so fast, she said, that no one would be able to stop her. Reports of the execution claimed that although the two men died quickly the execution of the woman was botched. The crowd was so intent watching the scene that the hangman was able to quietly disappear and was not seen again. Apparently the crowd wanted to find him and run him out of town on a rail.

Thus ended Sydney's only multiple execution and first murder drama. It was not its last although Mrs. Flahaven was the only Cape Bretoner to be executed on the island. There have been other executions but only, like Johnston and Easman, of those "from away".

RICHARD BROWN - WHEN COAL BECAME KING

Although not widely remembered today, few Englishmen have done more for Cape Breton than Richard Brown and his son. It was because of the efforts of Richard Brown senior, the first representative here of the General Mining Association (GMA), that coal mining became such an immense contributor to the economy of Nova Scotia. His son continued his father's efforts.

Coal had been mined on Cape Breton for more than a century when the General Mining Association obtained ownership of the leases. It had been dug from the cliffs where it outcropped by early sailors as early as 1715 and settlers took whatever coal they needed when it outcropped on their land. They had little regard for the niceties of the law and bootlegging, as it later became known, was widespread. The first Lieutenant Governor, DesBarres, had high hopes that royalties from the legal sales of coal would finance this new colony but he failed to take into account that the Navigation Laws restricted sale of coal to Halifax, a very small market. Nor could he raise money in England to capitalize the development of mines; the English were not going to help create a competitor to their own mines.

Coal mining in Britain developed rapidly in the late eighteenth and early nineteenth century, fueling the Industrial Revolution. A prominent mine owner, James Lowther, first earl of Lonsdale, who had enormous acreages in Cumberland, northwest England, boasted that he "owned the land, fire and water" in and around the port of Whitehaven. Man of letters and Earl of Orford, Horace Walpole, spoke disparagingly of him and described him as "the little contemptible tyrant of the north". James Lowther died in 1802 and the second earl was largely famous because of his friendship with the poet William Wordsworth rather than his mines. But of crucial importance for Cape Breton, Lowther sent one of his mine managers, Richard Brown, in those days called "a viewer", to Nova Scotia as chief engineer for the GMA which in 1826 acquired a sixty year monopoly over all the coal mines in the province.

Early in the GMA's operating period, and before, there was optimism that valuable reserves of copper could also be exploited. Britain was rife with rumour that Nova Scotia was teeming with mineral wealth. The Duke of York, who had initially owned the leases on minerals in the province, transferred those leases to a firm called Messrs. Rundell, Bridge and Rundell, Co, a well-known firm of jewelers and goldsmiths with large mining tracks in Columbia and Brazil. This company became, on completion the transfer, the General Mining Association. Plans were developed to mine the rumoured copper on an extensive scale and a Cornish mining engineer was sent to map the resource. When extensive surveys showed that the copper was probably not there these plans were abandoned and the GMA concentrated exclusively on coal mining.

Brown's instruction was to develop trade with the United States. In 1827 only 20% of the coal consumed in New York and Boston came from the UK, most of the rest being brought in from Pennsylvania and Virginia. The GMA failed to penetrate this market, largely because of tariff restrictions, but it did sell its steadily increasing production because of increasing demand in Canada. Coal production of about twenty thousand tons in 1825 had risen to one hundred thousand tons in the 1850s. This increase was largely due to the systematic exploitation of the coal resource under the management of Richard Brown, senior.

Brown was probably the first man to recognize the potential of Cape Breton's undersea coal resources. Much of the coal above sea level had been exhausted by earlier lessees so Brown had a shaft sunk close to the shore in an ambitious project to tunnel out under the ocean. This mine, on the Sydney seam, was called the New Winning, later the Princess. At the same time and in order to get some coal to the United States market, they would work a small portion of the seam still available above water level and estimated they could extract about ten thousand tons a year for two or three years. A community that mined coal from the Sydney Main seam developed and was called Sydney Mines. At first it was nicknamed "Lazytown". Apparently this was because local farmers, bringing their produce to market in the early hours of the morning, did not realize that a great number of the men were still asleep because they had been on shift work.

While mining this subterranean coal Brown had to have steam engines constructed to haul the coal to the surface and a railway built to carry it to the shore for further shipment to its ultimate market. The first piers for shipping coal were built in 1832 in the area known as the North Bar and a small community of homes began to appear around them. Two years later the railway from the mine to North Bar – now North Sydney – was completed with iron rails, called "fish bellies" brought from England. This line, some three miles in length and a similar railway in Pictou County, are believed to have been the first railways in North America built with iron rails. Horses pulled the coal cars up a slight grade for half the distance. Then they were unharnessed, put in an empty car at the end of the coal cars and the cars were allowed to glide down to the pier. Then the horses hauled the empty cars up the incline, were again unharnessed and the empty cars coasted back to the mine to be refilled. After twenty years of this two steam locomotives from England, named the "*Sydney*" and the "*Halifax*", replaced the horses.

After eight years of danger and difficulty the mine was opened. The coal was of excellent quality for domestic purposes, "igniting readily, burning freely and making a bright cheerful fire. The ashes are small in quantity, …settle under the grate, thereby leaving a clean tidy hearth in front of the fire." Capital investment had been considerable and the market in the United States never reached the optimistic expectations of the GMA and it was some years before the market markets in Canada developed and profits were realized. Nonetheless, Sydney coal had a high reputation as a steam coal. Until the Cunard ships stopped calling at Halifax they used Sydney coal for both their outward and home bound voyages. In the early years, before anthracite coal became available in the United States, their bituminous coal, aside from a small quantity of low grade coal from Virginia, was largely imported. But coal was not heavily used at that time; wood and charcoal were the most popular fuels, even for industrial uses in New England. As coal became more popular a canal, 108 miles long, brought anthracite coal from the central anthracite mining area to Philadelphia where it could be shipped at low cost and free of duty, to Boston and New

York. An additional constraint in penetrating the New York market concerned the sizing of coal. The GMA found that coal, large and small pieces mixed together could not be sold in New York since it had to compete with the more favored English coal which was carefully screened and hand picked for the New York market. Coal markets had to be developed in Canada.

Events in Britain, shortly before Brown came to Nova Scotia, were to have a profound impact on world coal mining. In 1812, while Britain was embroiled in its war with France and Napoleon planned his disastrous Russian campaign, there was a massive explosion in a mine in the north of England. The accident caused by a gas and dust explosion from miners using open flame lamps caused the deaths of ninety-two men and boys. National outrage resulted in colliery owners offering a substantial reward to anyone who could invent a safety lamp. Coal mining was expanding rapidly and shafts were driven still further underground to feed the growing demand for coal for industry and the needs of steam engines. The more rapidly coal was cut, the deeper the mines and poorer the ventilation, the greater the danger.

Early efforts to find a solution were unsuccessful so the owners approached the man regarded as the leading scientist in the country, Humphry Davy, director of the Royal Institution. Davy came north to investigate and stayed with John Buddle, head engineer of the West End Colliery. A few days later Davy left for his laboratory in the south. His parting words to Buddle were, "Do not despair, I think we can do something for you in a very short time." At the same time another inventor, George Stephenson, had been working on a solution to the problem. His lamp was tested successfully in the most dangerous areas of the mines and it worked. Meanwhile Davy had produced the first version of his lamp. Who was actually first in developing a lamp that could be used without danger in the mines is still debated but in January, 1816, John Buddle announced, "We have subdued the monster". Davy refused to take out a patent on his invention believing it wrong to charge a fee for something intended to save men's lives.

There were two classifications of "viewers", that is, engineers or mine managers. "Resident viewers", such as Richard Brown, senior, trained in England and a manager in the Lord Lonsdale's mines before coming to Cape Breton. "General viewers" such as John Buddle, could be in residence at a particular mine or could act as partners in a mining enterprise, or act as what we would today term as consultants. Buddle was regarded as the finest of colliery viewers and was commissioned in 1834 to write a report of the Sydney colliery. Buddle came to Sydney Mines and would have been of considerable value to Brown in the early development of the colliery there, in that he was able to help acquire iron coal tubs for the Sydney mines. That Brown continued to manage the GMA's operations on Cape Breton until his retirement indicates that Buddle's report to the British owners contained no serious criticism.

A letter Brown senior wrote to his son in 1877, who by this time had replaced his father as manager here, illustrates a continuing problem in management. The son had apparently complained that the GMA secretary was constantly involving himself in mine management matters. Brown senior replied that the GMA secretary had "been his cross to bear" and that secretaries attempted to justify their positions by investigating trifling matters of expense. The comment is one with a very modern ring.

Meanwhile Brown had a private side to his life. He married Sibella Barrington, daughter of Captain Barrington of the 60th Rifles and they had two daughters and four sons. He acquired a yacht, the *Adamant* and built a home on what came to be called Brown Street in Sydney Mines. As a geologist he was particularly interested in the fossil outcrops near Sydney Mines and wrote papers describing them in considerable detail. The cliffs at Sydney Mines are an illustration of evolution. There were once here vast forests which, over the millenniums had been compressed and submerged and during a period of unimaginable length became coal. Brown saw exposed on the cliffs the evidence of these "fossil forests" and studied them meticulously. His findings were published by the Geological Society in London that included among its members not only Richard Brown but also Charles Darwin. His name as a geologist has been compared with that of the Englishman, Sir Charles Lyell, and the Nova Scotian, Sir William Dawson.

Towards the end of his stay on Cape Breton Richard Brown was the Lieutenant Colonel in command of the militia. When, in 1860 the Prince of Wales visited Sydney Mines, Brown commanded the contingent that welcomed him. This was apparently unplanned. The two navy ships carrying the prince's party, *HMS Hero* and *HMS Ariadne*, had made faster than expected time leaving St. John's, Newfoundland on their way to Halifax. To take advantage of the gain the Royal party decided to stop at Sydney Mines to inspect the militia Volunteers under Brown's command. Afterwards the inspection the Prince, later King Edward VII, expressed a wish to see the Mi'kmaq encampment at Indian Beach. Horse and buggy drove him there. Most of the men were away for their annual ceremonies at Chapel Island. He was welcomed by the women there who gave him some of their handiwork. The royal party then drove on to North Bar (North Sydney) where another welcome awaited them. Fifty-two years later, long after both Browns were gone, the Governor-General of Canada, the Duke of Connaught, unveiled a monument to commemorate his brother's earlier visit. Also, it is said, that to commemorate the Prince's visit to Richard Brown's home, a golden spike was driven into the sill of the house. It is thought that this gold is no longer there.

In 1862 the GMA sent W.A. Hendry, assistant to the British Inspector of Mines, to report on operations in Nova Scotia and to ascertain whether Richard Brown's management had been efficient. He reported:

> Their underground works…are conducted with great regularity and scientific skill. My endeavor was, while inspecting the other collieries, to urge upon the proprietors the advantages – as far as circumstances would permit – of adopting the same system as that pursued by Mr. Brown, viz: to leave a regular and fair distribution of pillarage to support the roof or upper strata until the coal has been worked out from the extreme deep, when the pillars might be removed and the roof allowed to come down.

It is difficult today to judge if other mines were using the room and pillar method of extracting coal efficiently by the standards of the mid-eighteenth century. But what appears to be clear is that the GMA on Cape Breton, under the management of Richard Brown, wasted less coal than was usual in North American coal mining.

In June, 1864 Richard Brown resigned his position in favour of his son, Richard Brown, Junior. He returned to London. There, his commitment to Cape Breton continued. He wrote <u>The History of the Coal Fields and Coal Trade of Cape Breton</u> and <u>The History of the Island of Cape Breton.</u> He also continued to contribute his knowledge to the coal industry. Shortly before his resignation he wrote describing the details of a coal-hewing machine. Although the machine could be used only in a longwall operation, rather than the "board and pillar" used in Sydney Mines, his description, the details of its operation, including the pay rates of the sixteen operatives required, illustrate that even as he approached the end of his career, he kept his keen interest in advanced mining methods.

Brown senior was also aware of the differences between British and Nova Scotia mine management, particularly in regard to labour. Unlike Britain, labour scarcity was a factor in Nova Scotia. Here was a small population in relation to the large size of the mining operation. Attempts to improve the situation by importing labour were not always successful, although the skill level of miners had apparently improved after 1830. Prior to that most of the miners were from Newfoundland and were unskilled. In 1873, when Brown Junior was in charge, the provincial government tried to import French workers. In 1882 Brown senior wrote to his son deploring the "disgraceful conduct of scoundrels imported from Scotland". The labour problem was made worse because of mobility and miners were often prepared to move, often as a group, from coalfield to coalfield. But Brown senior also recognized that the needs of the workers had to be listened to and wrote in his book that the company had to provide the same rations and housing for all workers, regardless of their skill levels.

A case can be made that the GMA inhibited the development of industry on Cape Breton. Certainly the ownership of the leases on all Nova Scotia coal by one company would have eliminated the possibility of local people participating in ownership and development of mines; private entrepreneurship was inhibited up until 1967 because of offshore ownership of the two major local industries. Certainly also the British authorities were unlikely to support a tariff regime that would encourage colonial coal development to the detriment of British. That being said, however, there appears little doubt that Richard Brown, and later his son, did all within their power to create on Cape Breton an efficient coal industry.

THE LONELY LOVER – A TRAVELER'S TALE

Over the centuries scores of thousands have traveled to Cape Breton, some to stay briefly, some all their lives. In many cases, particularly during the early years of settlement, the men came first leaving wives and sweethearts to follow. This is the story of one young man named Clement of a strong religious inclination writing to Sarah his wife whom he had left two weeks earlier in Halifax. We do not know if he was a Brit or a Yank but feel that so romantic was his letter he must have been an Englishman. The year is 1849. The letter was sent from Sydney on 6 September recounting his journey after leaving Arichat. Not all is included but Clement's anguish at having received no letter from Sarah has a poignancy that can be appreciated today even though we now have telephones, airplanes and speedy land travel to shrink the distances. It may perhaps modify the image we have today of those stern Victorian gentlemen.

"Dear Sarah,

(First there are paragraphs on how we should give thanks to God, then,)

I am going to visit several places in this part of the island where there is a prospect of doing business, though I may perhaps deviate a little from my former plans.

Now for my progress since I last wrote you. The day after writing you was the Sabbath and I attended church morning and afternoon. In the evening I took tea at Dr. Fixott's where I saw one of the Miss Janes of Halifax who has been teaching music in Arichat. The evening seemed long and lonesome, no loved one beside me, to greet me with a kind and affectionate smile; no gentle pressure of the hand, a silent witness of inward emotion, none of those moments of indescribable happiness, of overflowing joy, which have been so often afforded me in the society of my dearly loved little Sarah. Oh you cannot imagine how much I miss my "pretty little wife", how necessary your presence is to my happiness. I could never be content to live at a distance from you for any length of time. I could bear almost anything except that, but away from you, everything appears dreary and black.

On Monday morning I packed up expecting to get away early in a boat bound to St. Peter's, but as it was blowing very hard they concluded to wait till afternoon. By the noon they were so "happy" as to be unfit for anything. The next morning I engaged my passage in another boat to start at ten o'clock. Ten o'clock came and she was not ready to start. The Captain said he expected to get going through the day as he was <u>very</u>

drunk. I declined waiting any longer and determined to try the lake tack. At first I could not get a horse, but Dr. Fixott very kindly, on hearing of my dilemma, came with his wagon and drove me to the Disgouse (sic) ferry, about eight miles, where I got a sail boat to take me over to St. Peter's. When I got there it was late in the afternoon and I still had about 70 miles to go and did not wish to wait another day, and as I could not get a vehicle of any kind, to start that evening got a man to row me six miles down the Bras D'Or lake to the Indian settlement where I engaged a canoe and two Indians to take me the rest of the way.

The scene of the Bras D'Or is most beautiful, some of it equal to anything in existence. When the moon rose about half past eight we started, and were soon gliding through the countless islands which throng the south end of the bay, some so completely shut in you could not perceive how you got in, or where you were going to get out and the water as smooth as glass. In a few moments we would turn perhaps to the left around one little point, and the next minute around another point to find ourselves again on the broad lake with a fresh breeze and a considerable sea running.

About ten o'clock, having threaded the most intricate and tortuous channel we hoisted sail and our frail little bark sped onwards over the crested billows with accelerated speed. The Indians alternatively slept and paddled but I kept my eyes open gazing upon the beautiful moonlit scene which spread around with ever varying aspect. Whenever I felt sleepy or cold I would paddle until I was well warmed and again sit down and quietly enjoy the scene, not without many vain wishes that my loved one was by my side, which would enhance each pleasurable feeling and make every scene far more lovely.

About half past six in the morning we came to the "Portage" or landing place about twelve miles by land from Sydney. Here we unloaded and one of the Indians took my trunk on his back, the other took the canoe on his head, I took the small arms and we crossed the Portage three miles where we embarked on a small lake and from there to Sydney had a most beautiful and romantic paddle you can conceive of for the distance of twelve miles. After crossing the lake we entered a brook which ran out of it winding among the trees in some places hardly wide enough for the canoe, in others rushing down a steep descent with scarcely enough water to float us. After some miles of this novel navigation, we came to the salt water but still for some miles more a beautiful river. I couldn't help planning some nice little excursion up that same river with a nice little girl I am acquainted with. After meeting the tide, which was running strong against us, as there was a nice breeze in our favour, and we had forgotten our mast and couldn't hoist sail, I hoisted my umbrella which helped the canoe along wonderfully....

Sydney is very prettily situated and pleases me more than any place I have visited. The people also are kind and the society better than most places of its size. I have already had some very kind offers of rides to the surrounding country. On Saturday I will accept one of them and visit the mines. I have also planned a fishing excursion for Monday next if my life is spared, up this same romantic river which I have described. I think I could pass a few weeks here very pleasantly, if it were not for the absence of one whose presence alone can enliven every scene and qualify them to inspire pleasure in me. Deprived of the light of my life, the sun of my existence, my cherub girl, the most beautiful scenery appears gloomy….. My dear Sarah, I can not find language to express one tithe of the depth and intensity of my love for you. Every thought, every motion, every wish and inspiration of my heart has your image connected with it, all have some reference to that object which has entwined itself around every sympathy of my nature and filled my heart with overflowing with its love."

This letter continues in a similar vein for a couple more paragraphs and ends with,

"God bless you dear Sarah and keep us both till we meet again and grant us a happy union,

Yours Sincerely.

Clement."

WILLIAM PENN HUSSEY - HUCKSTER

When the village of Salem, Massachusetts is spoken of today most people's memories will hark back to the infamous witchcraft trials of 1692. The former Salem Village was eventually absorbed into the town of Danvers that is close by the present town of Salem. Yet there are those who believe that some of the infamy of the Village of Salem survived and that a latter day resident was responsible for bewitching a number of wealthy investors and the community of Broad Cove on the western coast of Cape Breton Island.

Tales persist of the flamboyant career of William Penn Hussey and his impact on coal development in Inverness County, Cape Breton. Hussey was apparently an enormous man, not only gigantic in size but vast in self-esteem. Born in Berwick, Maine in 1847 by the time he was eighteen he was active in mining in California and when he returned to the east he established himself as a wholesaler and retailer of coal to the community. Apparently he soon amassed a small fortune. But small fortunes were not enough to satisfy his ambitions. He saw in the little developed coalfield off western Cape Breton an opportunity that, providing he could obtain the immense investment necessary, could propel him towards a very large fortune. The investment needs were considerable. Not only had he to mine the coal but a railway, a harbour and markets were also necessary.

Hussey impressed the locals with his visions of expansion and local prosperity, and also with his preposterous flamboyance. This enormous man, legend has it, rode round town on a large white horse, dressed as a cowboy, a pistol on each side of his gun belt and a six gallon hat on his head. He purchased the land for his coal development for $62,500 but needed far more.

Local legend also asserts that after attempting to float his scheme in Britain, France and Switzerland with some success he managed to persuade a wealthy industrialist from Zurich to cross the Atlantic to Broad Cove to see for himself the great opportunity. Hussey would leave nothing to chance. On the eastern side of the island, near New Waterford, it was possible to see some of the seams of coal outcropping on the cliff face. Not so on the western side where the seams run out under the seabed. Hussey is said to have made every effort to convince the Swiss industrialist and hired several workers to paint some of the nearby walls of rock black. When the Swiss investor looked from the deck of his ship he marveled at what he saw and, it is said, immediately told Hussey he would invest a million dollars.

In the winter of 1894 the Broad Cove Coal Company was incorporated. Hussey was manager and treasurer of the company. He had a narrow gauge railway from the coal pits to the harbour, two miles away, and the coal was stored there until vessels from eastern Canada and Maine arrived to load it. New investment arrived in the village and the community grew. The element of hucksterism remained. As late as 1904 the local newspaper, The *Inverness News*, said that Hussey's enterprise "ranked among the richest coal mines in the world". William Penn Hussey had been actively assisted by his son, J. Fred Hussey who had installed compressed air mining equipment and improved the productivity. But when his father talked of selling the company he knew that his time there was limited as well.

Both Husseys left in 1899, back to their home in Danvers never to return to Cape Breton. Local opinion was divided about the benefits they left behind. Some thought they had benefited the area by developing a community. Most thought they had gouged the area and had done nothing beyond what was necessary to pull out the greatest profit for them. The local papers of the times were fulsome in their praise and ecstatically reported the high esteem in which the Hussey family was held. A formal address on behalf of the people of Broad Cove to J. Fred Hussey spoke of his "energy, honor, and success by yourself and your worthy father" while "you were ever careful to see that the men who worked for you were properly treated and properly paid" and that "you have earned the respect and gratitude of the people of Broad Cove, who will never cease to pray for your future health and happiness." It is not without significance that these words were written by the Hussey company solicitor.

The Husseys retired to a mansion style home called Riverbank in Danvers. In 1902 William Penn on the occasion of Danvers 150th anniversary rode his horse at the head of a parade which was said to have taken six hours to pass. The event and all the bands in it were financed by W. P. Hussey. When he died in 1910, at the age of sixty-three, his last wishes were not respected. Apparently he made it known that he wished his body to be mummified and placed in a glass case

They Came From Away

and displayed in a standing position on the lawn at Riverbank. . It was not to be. Instead he was buried in a park close to his home.

Today Riverbank still stands at 154 Water Street in Danvers but now it is owned by the New England Home for the Deaf. Across the street is an equestrian statue showing Hussey as Chief Marshall of the 1902 Danvers 150th anniversary parade. Coal is no longer mined at Broad Cove.

PHILIP WORGAN

""Ferndell" the beautiful residence of Captain P.H. Worgan, RNR, King's Road, was the scene last evening of one of the most brilliant social events that has taken place in Sydney for some time, when their daughter Miss Gwendolyn was united in the bonds of matrimony to Mr. T.H. Creden, the popular general manager of the CB Electric Co."

So wrote the *Sydney Record* in December, 1903. What followed was a lengthy description of the house, the guests and, odd to modern ears, a description of the presents given by the various guests to the bride and groom. Later that evening, wrote the *Record*, the bride and groom drove in a sleigh drawn by several young men of the party to the siding below Captain Worgan's residence where a special train with Pullman and baggage car attached, was awaiting the happy couple.

Much writing about Cape Breton focuses on the harsh life suffered or endured by new arrivals to the island and the confrontational nature of relations between management and labour. There was much hardship. Life certainly had its seamy side, particularly in Sydney after the opening of the steel plant. There was plenty of confrontation. It was not exclusive to this island but was general throughout North America and Europe. The Industrial Revolution was not a kindly affair. While Cape Breton miners and steel workers struggled to better their working conditions and increase the wages of labour, much the same was happening in packing plants of Chicago, the coal mines of Appalachia and the sweat shops of New York. Mayor A. D. Gunn complained in his 1913 report that the health statistics were alarming and that some of the streets were like mud filled trenches. Many people bore the brunt of the effects of rapid industrial expansion. But not all.

Concentration on the harsh aspects of life here has tended to cloud the fact that in Sydney and elsewhere on the island there were residents who lived a life both gentle and genteel and also that the less affluent had their entertainments.

Among the more prosperous families in the industrial area of Cape Breton there were the Dodds and the Burchells, the Ingrahams and Crawleys, the McLennans and the Kendalls. One family that illustrated some of the more gracious aspects of life was that of the Worgans.

Philip Worgan was a young Royal Navy officer when he first came to Cape Breton in 1866, something of a veteran. He was serving on *HMS Wolverine* that had just played a small part in the brutal suppression of a revolt in Jamaica. One alleged rebel, George William Gordon, was taken on board the *Wolverine*, at that time apparently commanded by Sub-Lieutenant Worgan, was transported to Morant Bay and hanged. The entire handling of the uprising and the savagery by which it was repressed, caused outrage in Britain, particularly over the hanging of Gordon against whom there appeared to be little evidence. There were efforts to have the governor tried for murder but although he was replaced as governor no further action was taken against him.

Philip Worgan, however, appears to have come out of these unhappy events with an untarnished reputation. According to his biography he was captain of the *Wolverine* at the time of the revolt and received a letter on commendation from members of the black community on the island. He had, said the letter, intervened when two black men were about to be hanged. The ropes were already around their necks but Worgan stopped the execution so that a proper trial could take place. They were later acquitted. Half a dozen black Jamaicans, led by Robert Gordon, Headmaster of Wolmer's Grammar School in Kingston, signed the fulsome letter.

Philip Worgan was born in Lancashire in 1843, the son of the Reverend John and Phillipa Worgan. The Royal Navy College at Dartmouth in England did not open until 1863 when Worgan was twenty and those destined to be officers would have entered naval service at that time joined between the ages of twelve and fifteen. Assuming that Worgan was fifteen when he joined, in 1858, he would have gone straight to sea and received his training on board. In 1859 a training ship, the *Britannia*, was established but the likelihood is that Worgan would have been too old to go to it. Joining the Royal Navy at so young an age would certainly have given him a great sense of responsibility and self-confidence. Worgan's biography refers to his service aboard the *HMS Lee* and visiting Mediteranian ports from Morocco to Alexandria and Bierut. This practical experience was further enhanced during the American Civil War when the *Wolverine* was on blockade duties off the United States. After serving some years as a midshipman he was then promoted to sub-lieutenant, the rank he held on the *Wolverine*.

The Jamaica rebellion over, the *Wolverine* sailed north on its way home to England. It stopped first in Halifax, then Sydney and sub-lieutenant Worgan took shore leave. It was then that he met the twenty year old, Annie Blackadar. When Worgan reached England he was "paid off", that is, he went on the reserve of officers since the Royal Navy was going through one of its many cutbacks. He then returned to Cape Breton and on 11 December, 1871 married Annie Blackadar at St George's Church. Soon after he purchased the Ferndell farm on King's Road that had been owned by relatives of Miss Blackadar. The farm had fifty-three acres of land stretching above King's Road and down to the harbour shore. The farmhouse, which earlier had been owned by Richard Gibbon, son of the first Chief Justice of Cape Breton, was built from stone rescued from the dismantled Louisbourg Fortress.

Soon Worgan was making additions to the house and it became an elegant and impressive structure containing antique furniture bought at auctions and Worgan's service souvenirs. It was not as grand as the soon to be built Moxham Castle but in the memories of those who lived there it combined elegance with warm homeliness. It also became a centre of social life, particularly as Philip Worgan became involved in local civic and church administration.

The Worgan house was not the only one of distinction. In Westmount was the Ingraham house with its broad staircase, high ceilinged reception rooms and fireplaces in all the bedrooms and the McLennan home of newspaper owner and industrialist Senator McLennan. At the turn of the century came Moxham Castle on King's Road, overawing the Worgan estate and challenging the social supremacy of the Northside. In all these homes social life celebrated the confidence of the late nineteenth and early twentieth centuries. Music and dance had shed some of their earlier formality. In 1899 the big hit was "After the Ball" and with the South African War came the poignant "Goodbye Dollie Gray". The great fire of Sydney in 1901, which gutted the wooden heartland of the town only briefly dampened the sense of optimism prevailing. Soon new buildings were rising, made of brick this time. The social life of King's Road, Westmount and Sydney's Northend flourished.

Of course, people did not have parties for their own sakes. Some excuse, far fetched perhaps, was needed for a celebration that would shorten the winter months; a wedding or anniversary at any time of the years was good for celebration.

In Sydney a great opportunity to socialize came with the visits of naval ships. One visit in particular, in November of 1903, of the Italian warship, the *Carlo Alberto*, resulted in a major celebration. The *Sydney Record* became quite lyrical in its description "– amid the strains of exquisite music, the mirth and laughter of merry dancers and the picturesque character of the ballroom decorations" - and made quite sure that the name of every guest and the description of the dresses of every young woman present were included. Those present included the Worgans, the Dodds and the Ingrahams, the Kimbers and the Murrays, the Burchills and the Crowes. Even the Horsfalls were there, bravely facing critics of their school in Westmount. The centre of the celebration aboard the ship was the inventor Guglielmo Marconi. The *Sydney Record* let the public know that Mrs. Dodd wore gray silk trimmed with black lace and jet while Miss Edith Worgan wore lavender voile, her sister Mabel pale blue silk. Mrs. Arnold Foster was in black and one must wonder, in retrospect if that colour had anything to do with the presence of the Horsfalls. Their host was Captain Martini and his officers, the music was provided by the Cibou Orchestra and as midnight approached the guests gathered around Mr. Marconi to be photographed for posterity.

The arrival of naval vessels had often been the occasion for celebration. In July, 1899 the Sydney Carnival was held with hundreds of people from the outlying areas coming to town to join in and the Sydney to Louisbourg train itself brought in two hundred passengers. The fleet was in town. While the band played in Victoria Park and the population picnicked the English Man-of-war the *Crescent* commanded by Vice Admiral Sir F.G.D. Bedford sailed in at the head of a flotilla that included the *Prosperine*, the *Indefatigable* and the torpedo destroyer, the *Quail*. Close by the cannons of Commodore Henrique's French warship the *Isley* boomed out their salute while the harbour itself was jammed with an array of pleasure boats.

The arrival of ships into Sydney Harbour always seems to have been accompanied by festivities. Since the Treaty of Paris had ended the American War of Independence, French men o' war visited Sydney every year – except when the Napoleonic Wars were in progress. They anchored near the home of the John Bourinot, the French consul – close by where the Marine Terminal and the Big Fiddle are now – and when the admiral's ship was in bands were sent on shore and gave concerts outside Senator Bourinot home where "the youth and beauty of the town could be seen promenading with the officers in their gay uniforms". Frequently dinners and dances were given on shore and the French officers returned the hospitality aboard their ships.

Weddings were a more frequent occasion for celebration and the newspaper informed the public not just of the event itself but often included a detailed list of those present and the gifts they gave to the bride and groom. Consequently, at the Worgan wedding the guests could later rate their own gifts against those of others.

Philip Worgan probably had private money, something not unusual, indeed almost mandatory for many British army and naval officers at that time. But he was active in civic affairs – and became Sydney's second mayor – and in church matters. At the wedding of his daughter, described earlier, the Reverend Mr. Woodroofe officiated assisted by the Venerable Archdeacon Smith D.D. St. Mark's Church at Coxheath was built in 1892 under the leadership of Philip Worgan and Archdeacon Smith. The Worgans regularly attended St George's but perhaps found St Mark's closer.

Churches were frequently the focus of social events, festivities were widespread and far from confined to the wealthier inhabitants. Picnics were held throughout the summer, there was swimming at the beaches, boating in the harbour, skating and ice sailing in the winter and train rides were taken to Iona in the summer with picnics on the shore before the journey home. While the social leaders of the area had their weddings and other festivities reported in the press the general public enjoyed itself as well.

HENRY MELVILLE WHITNEY - "FINDER OF SYDNEY"

No one, before or since, has had so great an impact on the economy of Cape Breton than Henry Melville Whitney.

Whitney, a successful American entrepreneur, came to Cape Breton in 1893 looking for an inexpensive source of coal to power his enterprises in Boston - the West End Street Railway Company, the largest electrical rail system in North America at that time, and his Metropolitan Steamship Company.

He was not a young man at the time; fifty-four years old, he was both by birth and achievement an established member of America's "Gilded Age" aristocracy. The Whitneys were power brokers in old Boston. Henry's father's enterprises included chartering steamboats to the government and he was president of the only bonded steamship line between Boston and New York. Henry worked for his father but struck out on his own in and after the American Civil War, soon speculating in the south in cotton and in raising sunken shipping. As those opportunities faded he came north again to the security of his father's operations and by the time he was thirty-five owned a substantial portion of the family business as well as considerable real estate.

Only three weeks after his marriage at the age of thirty-nine, Henry's father died and Whitney inherited the presidency of the Metropolitan Steamship Company. He was also a major player in the West End Street Railway and bought into other streetcar companies believing an integrated rail system would benefit his own holdings as well as the community. The time was ripe. In 1887 horses were still the main source of power and Whitney needed ten thousand of them. They were slow and inefficient, as well as expensive to maintain. Whitney was well aware of work being done to develop electricity and was convinced that electrification of the rail transit system would succeed. Soon the Brookline-Boston section of his own West End Street Railway became the largest of its type in North America.

To produce electricity to run streetcars or anything else needed coal, more than was then available to him. The nearest cheap source was Cape Breton. Encouraged by Nova Scotia Premier Fielding – later federal finance minister – he pursued his project of purchasing Cape Breton mines. In conjunction with Halifax lawyer B.F. Pearson options were acquired on the mines. Whitney knew that by consolidating the management of these previously diverse operations he could cut costs and increase operating efficiency. Government support was substantial and in 1892 the provincial government offered him a ninety-nine year lease, an attractive royalty and was also prepared to heavily subsidize the costs of building a new railway between Sydney, Glace Bay and Louisbourg.

The new mining methods were efficient as promised. Endless haulage ropes, cutting machines and larger coal cars were brought in for this new Dominion Coal Company and a coal washing plant was built. By 1901 production of more than 2.5 thousand tons was three times what the mines had brought to the surface in 1893. There was plenty of criticism. There was the usual complaint that management really knew nothing about mining. There were fears that the pricing structure was designed to make Whitney's other enterprises appear profitable at the expense of coal.

Whitney's energy propelled him into other enterprises such as the Halifax Electric Tramway Company, the Halifax Street Railway Company, the Nova Scotia Power Company and the Halifax Illuminating and Motor Company. Soon iron and steel attracted him. He had talked with steelmaker Arthur Moxham and intrigued him with ideas of further consolidation. Whitney had the coal, limestone was nearby and he had acquired two thirds of the Belle Island, Wabana iron ore fields in Newfoundland. Now Moxham would agree not only to invest in a new steel plant, totally integrated, but would manage it as well.

The new steel plant was at the cutting edge of technology with its integrated facilities all under one roof. The team that created the Dominion Iron and Steel Company (DISCO) was impressive. It included plant designer Julian Kennedy, well known in the industry who had just returned from Russia where he had been in charge of construction of a large iron works. The Board of Directors included men such as Almeric Paget, president of the Chihuahua and Pacific Railway, H.F. Dimock, a governor of Yale University and manager of the Metropolitan Steamship Company, William Van Horne from Montreal, famous for his role in the construction of the Canadian Pacific Railway, Robert Mackay, president of Bell Telephone of Canada, and John S. McLennan, treasurer of Dominion Coal who would later own and edit the *Sydney Post* and write a book about Louisbourg Fortress that influenced its reconstruction.

From the beginning the optimism was tarnished by reality. Impurities in the iron ore made production of pig iron difficult. Local coal had a high sulphur and ash content causing excessive temperatures and frequent and costly relining of the open heath furnaces. Lack of capital prevented the roll mill being completed on time. Lack of skilled workers locally meant their importation from away. Initial targets for rail production of three thousand tons a day had to be reduced to one thousand tons a day for the Canadian market only. There were labour problems. Indebtedness increased. By November, 1901, Whitney has seen the trend. He sold controlling interest in the steel company to Montreal financiers.

Years later the *New York Times* would write, "As the organizer of the Dominion Coal Company, from which grew the present coal and iron industry of Cape Breton, Nova Scotia, it has been said of him that 'no American ever did more for Canada'" Today, more than a hundred years after his achievements, he is not well remembered. Prophetic words were written in 1900. "In the distant future – very distant – it is hoped when the last vestige of the steel works will have vanished, Whitney Avenue will help to remind future Sydneyites of the man who, if not the founder, was at least the finder of Sydney"

ARTHUR J. MOXHAM – BUILDER OF STEEL PLANTS AND STONE CASTLES

It was to be a grand but private social occasion in New York. Gathered together at the palatial home of Henry Whitney and his wife were the directors of the Dominion Iron and Steel Company (DISCO). They were Henry Whitney himself and his brother, William, New Yorkers Henry Dimock and Almeric Paget, John S MacLellan from Boston, David MacKeen from Halifax, the railroad builder from Montreal, Sir William Van Horne, and from Sydney, Nova Scotia, Arthur J. Moxham. Some were with their wives and all were looking forward to the social gathering that evening to end an intense day of business discussion.

It did not occur. During the afternoon the arrival of a telegram interrupted the conference. It was from Sydney for Arthur Moxham. It contained terrible news that sent him hurrying back to Cape Breton by special train and cancelled all socializing at The Whitneys' home.

For the first time in Arthur Moxham's career there was a crisis that he could do nothing to control or alleviate.

Something of a mystery hovers in the background of Arthur J. Moxham. Nothing to discredit him for sure, but enough to make an inquirer wonder why a boy of only fifteen years, from a socially established family, should turn his back on family and community to set off by himself across the Atlantic from Britain to the United States of America.

Young Moxham's hometown was Neath, near Swansea in Wales. It was a town with an established reputation for high quality copper and lead smelting and also had extensive tinplate, steel and galvanized sheet works as well as iron and brass foundries, steam engine factories, engineering works and chemical production plants. It was prosperous.

Arthur Moxham's family was less prosperous, but was socially prominent, although the family was said, in the cliché of the times, to be "in reduced circumstances". The Moxham boy had a natural bent for engineering and lived in a community where such a bent could be put to good use. Nonetheless, his family thought he could not learn a trade in town without damaging their social standing. Was it youthful ambition, family snobbery or both that sent this fifteen year old across the Atlantic? Whatever, Britain's loss was soon to be America's gain.

Moxham had an advantage greater than that of most immigrants. Dora Morgan was his aunt, his mother's sister, and the second wife of Thomas Coleman Sr. president of the Louisville Rolling Mill. She got him his job there.

The boy began working in America at a rolling mill in Louisville, Kentucky as a receiving clerk but quickly acquired practical experience in all aspects of the business. In the financial panic of 1873 the company went into receivership and Moxham and some friends were able to lease the works and run it successfully. The re-financing came from Fred Du Pont – the Du Ponts and the Colemans were related by marriage. At about the same time Arthur Moxham married Helen Coleman, the president's daughter. Five years later Moxham saw the industrial opportunities of the new town of Birmingham in Alabama. Five years after the end of the Civil War, Birmingham was little more than a large cotton field where two major railways met and the later city was a result of promotion by a railway sponsored land company. When Moxham went there in 1875 the population had not yet reached three thousand. Recognizing the potential of the limestone and iron ore deposits of the region, he organized and built the Birmingham Rolling Mills Company. This doubled the town's population. Another entrepreneur, Tom L. Johnson, wanted to produce rails suitable for street railroads and tramways. He approached the now twenty-six year old Moxham. Out of this meeting grew the Johnson Company, located at Johnstown, Pennsylvania, and soon to become the world's largest manufacturer of street railway supplies.

Moxham had been in the city a short while and would have been quite unaware, as were other citizens, of the ultimate results of the purchase by the local hunting and fishing club of a dam a dozen miles above the city. This club was a resort for the wealthy. It had only around sixty members but included among them were Andrew Carnegie, Andrew Mellon and Henry Clay Frick who has been described as "the most despised man in America". The dam was built in 1852 to create a storage reservoir for the Pennsylvania canal. It was seven hundred feet long and one hundred feet high and created the Conemaugh Lake. On 31 May, 1889 after ten inches of rain in twenty four hours the dam gave way. A wall of water three stories high swept over Johnstown almost completely destroying the city. The Pennsylvania railroad bridge held, but masses of debris piled up against it covering several acres. Many residents were saved from drowning by scrambling into the debris but then it caught fire and many were burnt alive.

The Johnstown flood resulted in the deaths of well over two thousand people. The now thirty-five year old Moxham showed his mettle and a U.S. Congressman later said of him, "This man Moxham is not a citizen of the United States, but he is a resident of Johnstown; they know him there, and when that fearful flood swept down; when after that awful night twelve thousand people were left without food or shelter and the sun rose on three thousand corpses, it was this Englishman, Arthur J. Moxham, who at the first gathering of survivors was by common acclaim made dictator. It was he who at that dreadful moment stepped to the front and, in the name of the whole community brought order out of chaos – who destroyed the whiskey and seized food, who fed the living and buried the dead and again set in motion the machinery of organized government and civilized life."

The plant at Johnstown became highly successful and Moxham and his partner decided that instead of purchasing steel they would produce it. The Lorain Steel Company was founded in Lorain, Ohio, on the southside of Lake Erie, with Arthur Moxham as its president.

By 1899 Moxham, now forty-five years old, was wealthy. The time had come for him to retire. He traveled to England, purchased a steam yacht and made plans to tour the world. After a summer of cruising with his wife and their four children as well as with his wife's parents, he landed at New York where he met with Henry Melville Whitney. He had known Whitney known from the days when Whitney was president of Boston's West End Electric Railway. Whitney had plans percolating and persuaded Moxham to come with him to Sydney, Nova Scotia, to look at its potential. Moxham, a hands-on industrialist was probably chaffing at the bit at an unwelcome retirement and sent for his brother, a mining engineer who had later emigrated from Wales. Edgar made an extensive and positive report and Moxham agreed to invest in a new steel plant and become its first general manager and vice president. The plant, on Sydney Harbour, had easy access to coal from local mines, nearby limestone and iron ore from Belle Isle, Newfoundland.

There was a glitch in the plans. On retirement Arthur and his wife, Helen, had decided that in addition to sailing the world they would build a beautiful home in Lorain, Ohio, scene of their greatest and, so he thought, final industrial triumph. Helen was tired of constant travel. After a life of living in construction camps, hotel rooms and other people's houses she wanted a place of her own. So Arthur Moxham built her dream home, evocative of a Scottish mansion. Helen wanted to stay there. Arthur, still only forty-seven years old, may still have had ambitions. And Henry Melville Whitney was persuasive. What he was offering Moxham was charge of the first great modern blast furnace and open-hearth plant in Canada. It was to be a totally integrated steel plant with four coke oven batteries, four blast furnaces, ten open hearth furnaces, blooming mill, billet mill and was laid out for a rod mill, rail mill, bar mill, plate mill and wire and nail mill.

Moxham accepted the challenge and to placate his wife, who wanted to stay home in Lorain in her beautiful new home, built a duplicate in Sydney, on King's Road where Cabot House now stands adjacent to Day's Inn. In its glory days this thirty-room castle had a large, stone-pillared porch opening into the grand main hall, a winding staircase leading to the thirty bedrooms. In addition to the kitchen there was a butler's pantry, breakfast nook, a sewing room, billiard room, small dining room, main dining room, den, living room, a library and two cloakrooms and a tower. Attached to the main house was a conservatory with flowers and goldfish. The grounds outside were generously landscaped with groves of birch, elm, maple and walnut trees imported from Europe. Adjacent to the house was the gatehouse – the only part of the Moxham building which still survives. The outer shell of the "castle" - it was soon named "Moxham's Castle" by Sydney residents - was constructed of stone taken from the abandoned fortress at Louisbourg but virtually all the internal items were brought from their home in Lorain.

The Moxhams had five children. The oldest, named Thomas Coleman, was twenty-four years old in 1901. He had married Ellen Huston the year before. Next was Egbert, at that time studying electrical engineering at Cornell University. Arthur and Helen's daughter Florence was born in Johnstown but died a week later. The two other daughters were Dulcenia, just married to Ellen Huston's brother, and Evangeline, called "Amy". As was typical of the great industrial families of that era, family linkages were strong. For example, Arthur Moxham's brother, Edgar, married Bessie Coleman, Helen Johnson's sister. Sadly, she died after the birth of their third child.

Thomas C. Moxham worked at the steel plant that in 1901 was in the construction phase. Tom, as superintendent of plant construction felt he should be on the job first thing in the morning. After breakfast on the morning of 5 June he took his chestnut standard-bred gelding from the stable and, at a quick canter went along King's Road, past the site of the new court house, then to George Street, Muggah's Creek bridge and the DISCO works. He stabled his horse then went to the blooming mill. He had a busy morning at his office and then, after lunch returned to the blooming mill.

Around four that afternoon he was where the locomotives were pushing dump carts heavy with rock fill. He signaled the driver of one of the locomotives that he wanted to board the car. When it approached he grabbed the handrail and went to step onto the footboard. He must have slipped. He fell beneath the wheels of the car and was killed instantly. Workers nearby were powerless to help. The plant doctor was sent for. Nothing could be done and the body was transferred to the hospital.

That night close to two hundred men marched together to the Moxham home to pay their respects to the family. Inside, three ministers, one priest, Mayor Crowe, friends, company executives and servants sought to console the family. An urgent wire was sent to Arthur at the Whitney home in New York and another to Egbert at Cornell University.

The same evening Arthur Moxham, on a special train heading north, was joined by Egbert who had come down from Ithaca to accompany his father. When the train reached Sydney it stopped on the grounds below the Moxham home and Arthur and Egbert left their private car to be met by their family, the Mayor and the company doctor.

The following day the train left Sydney and once again stopped at the grounds below Moxham's Castle. The coffin was placed in the car behind the engine and after that the private car was reserved for the family. Hundreds of residents of Sydney crowded the castle grounds and in silence watched the Moxhams leave. Arthur returned once more to Sydney, basically to close his involvement with the company. Tom's wife, "Honey" Moxham also stayed behind. Local legend has it that on hearing the news of his death she fell down the stairs. Whether this was true or not she remained in Sydney because she was seven months pregnant. She died two months later and her child was stillborn. The other Moxhams never came back. It is believed that the Arthur and Helen Moxham were distraught at their cumulative losses. They had lost their son, their daughter in law and their first grandchild. The spirit had gone out of them. The home, their castle, was abandoned and all the furnishings left behind for the next occupant.

Arthur Moxham joined the Du Pont Corporation as a member of its first Executive Committee. He had long been associated with the Du Ponts both as a friend and a valued business advisor. After instituting major reorganization of the company and finding new outlets for Du Pont products he resigned in 1913 to head the Aetna Explosives Company. He died in 1931. Helen Moxham, once known as "Happy Helen", went into a state of constant mourning. Neither returned to Lorain to live but to a home in Great Neck, Long Island, New York. She died in 1932.

During the First World War Moxham's Castle was used as a military hospital for returning veterans where they could rest and recuperate. Later it was used as a backdrop in the making of two films. For some years it was the private residence of a local shipping magnate, after which it was left vacant. It became a target for vandalism and on 25 April, 1966 it was destroyed by fire.

The steel plant, pride of Whitney and source of anguish for the Moxhams, also declined. After abandonment by Hawker Siddeley owners in 1967 it became a provincial Crown Corporation gradually accumulating a massive debt load. It ended its century long existence in 2002.

ONE OF MANY

At about the same time that the funeral cortège left Sydney with the body of Tom Moxham aboard, an elderly gentleman was on his way to the steel plant from Conception Bay, Newfoundland. He had traveled, possibly on an ore carrying boat from Belle Island or more likely on the *SS Bruce* from Port aux Basques, in order to see his son who, like so many young Newfoundlanders had headed to "the mainland" in search of better financial opportunities. A job at the steel plant was certainly regarded as one of those better opportunities.

The son was Archibald Russell from Conception Bay and it is likely that he too had reached Sydney on an ore boat from Belle Island or possibly on the *SS Bruce*.

Legend has it that the iron ore necessary for steel production had been discovered quite by chance. One story said that a fisherman had found a block of ore on Belle Island and was using "killick", a cradle filled with rocks as the anchor. While he was in St. John's harbor this was discovered and as a result the huge deposits of ore on Belle Island, in Conception Bay, were revealed. Another story was that Newfoundland schooners used to dump their ballast in Sydney Harbour. They used the red rock as ballast since it was noticeably heavier. Gradually an island of rock arose, became known as "Newfoundland Island" and some bright person had it analyzed and the source traced. Yet another story was that someone on Belle Island gave a few pounds of the red rock as a sample to a British sea captain to have it analyzed in England. Later the captain wrote back asking for fifty pounds more. They thought he meant fifty pounds sterling and ignored the request.

Whatever events led to its commercialization, the Nova Scotia Steel Company reportedly paid the Butler family, $120,000 for the whole property and they then sold a portion off to Whitney's Dominion Iron and Steel Company for a million dollars. The site of the mine on Belle Island was named Wabana, apparently an Indian word meaning "Where the light shines", but for the boys working from as young as ten years to separate the rocks from the ore the light must have seemed dim at best. For the men as well; in August, 1896, they went on strike for twelve cents an hour – a raise of two cents. One hundred years of steel production on Cape Breton began.

People poured into the island from across the world and among the many were Newfoundlanders in search of economic betterment. Life in rural Newfoundland was hard, harder even than that of Cape Breton for the winters are longer and the cold damper. People lived off the land; like here they had a garden, a cow and a horse for ploughing and the women were usually responsible for the garden and cow. Initially the settlers were called "planters" but the term should not suggest that they aspired to plantations in the sense that those existed in the southern United States. They were not proprietary owners of great tracts of land but simply those engaged in the resident fishery as opposed to those who came to Newfoundland annually to fish and then returned to Britain. Agricultural opportunity was limited. Cape

Breton raised about twice as much livestock in the mid-nineteenth century as the entire colony of Newfoundland and a couple of Cape Breton counties yielded twice the hay. Conception Bay life was a hard life but they leaned the skills of fishermen. At certain times of the year the men could go to "the Labrador" fishing cod and, in the spring, sealing. Those living near Brigus and Conception Bay worked logging or building roads and there was work to be had building and developing the railway. The more adventurous headed down to New York City where they worked in the construction industry on the high-rise buildings – they had the reputation of having no fear of heights. The young women sometimes became domestic workers in the homes of the wealthier "merchant" families in St. John's and sent their earnings home.

Cape Bretoners had a little more variety. They often joined the "harvest trains" heading west in the summer while daughters headed down to "the Boston States" for domestic work. Cash income was eagerly sought by both Newfoundlanders and Cape Bretoners.

By 1902 the surface iron ore at Wabana had been largely depleted. The mining went underground. Perhaps, and this must be entirely speculative, Archibald Russell's father thought that if his son could come home not only could he get a good job in this developing mine, possibly equal in pay to the one in Sydney's steel plant, but if at anytime he were laid off he could work in the woods or go fishing with others in the family. So he set off for Sydney, possibly on an ore boat, to give his son the good news.

When Russell senior arrived in Sydney the despondency of the town was apparent. The evening before a delegation of two hundred of steel workers walked to "Moxham Castle" on King's Road to express their condolences to the Moxham family on the tragic loss of their son, Tom, the day before.

Russell senior arrived at the gates of the steel plant but he was, in accordance with the regulations, refused admission. He decided to wait outside the gate until his son came off the shift at 6pm. But at 4.30 that afternoon a small group came through the gates. They were carrying the body of Archibald Russell. Shortly before, while Archibald Russell was working at the open hearth "the purchase of a block fastened at some height above him gave way and the block in its fall struck him on the head. His skull was broken and his death almost instantaneous". Archibald Russell was in his thirties and had worked at the steel plant for some time. He was a member of the Salvation Army and the following evening, a Sunday, a service was held for him at the Salvation Army barracks in Sydney. His father accompanied the body back to St John's aboard the *SS Bruce* as far as Port Aux Basques and then on by rail, a rail line of 558 miles that had been completed just three years earlier.

This sad event was just one of more to follow. Records were not well kept at that time, but in 1901 there were ten violent deaths in Sydney, among them other Newfoundlanders. Earlier, in January William Peddle of Spanish Bay died. A week later Kenneth Morse of Trinity Bay died in an explosion and six months later John Holley, also from Conception Bay died.

Archibald Russell's death made a little note in the history of Cape Breton. His was the first instance in which the jury agreed that the accident was caused by the carelessness of mine officials.

BLACK STEELWORKERS FROM ALABAMA

At the beginning of the twentieth century Sydney was a morning star in the economic development of Canada. What had recently been a sleepy colonial town overshadowed by its neighbour, North Sydney, was transformed by the coming of the steel plant. This plant would dominate the economy of Sydney for the next one hundred years and the explosion of population caused by the influx of workers to the plant totally change the region.

Would-be steel workers came from as near as the rural counties to as far as Eastern Europe, and from Newfoundland and the United States.

Unskilled workers were found and quickly given some training. Skilled workers were harder to find. Immigration policies were not as stringent as today and people poured into Canada from around the globe. In Canada between 1901 and 1911 the population increased by 34%. Sydney in 1891 had a population of 2,427. Twenty years later it had reached 17,723. A great air of optimism gripped the city. The steel plant needed coal and this caused a major increase in production from the local mines. The resulting prosperity saw a rapid increase in the local infrastructure. A massive fire that gutted the heart of the city in 1901 prompted new construction of brick.

There was a feeling that Sydney was on the brink of great prosperity. But much new development in areas of the city close to the steel plant where immigrant workers settled was often squalid and the squalor resulted in sickness and death. For example, near the steel plant for every four births one child died; in the more established parts there was one death for every thirteen births.

Although not explicitly stated in the regulations, immigration into Canada by non-whites was discouraged. Chinese immigrants headed for Vancouver and work on the railways. They were not welcomed in eastern Canada. Many Blacks faced constraints on their immigration into Canada. Blacks from the West Indies overcame some of these constraints. Would-be immigrants from Barbados traveled illegally on small schooners in the coal and molasses trade and were dropped off near Port Hawkesbury, where there were no immigration officials, and then made their way to the industrial region of the island.

Yet one group of black workers was encouraged. These included experienced steel workers from Alabama. They were brought in with the encouragement of plant management, initially largely American, so that they could act as foremen and train local and immigrant unskilled workers. Plant management, particularly an early Superintendent of Furnaces, John Means whose family was involved with the Means Fulton Iron Works of Birmingham, Alabama, recognized the value of their experience as blast furnace iron workers. The local attitude, however, conformed to stereotypes. The local explanation was that only Blacks could stand the heat of the blast furnaces. Black workers from Alabama were treated by management as skilled men but those from the West Indies were seen strictly as labourers.

Whatever management thought of the men from Alabama there appears to have been distinct prejudice against them in the community. There was also uncertainty as to how long they were expected to stay and possibly they were only wanted until replacements from Europe arrived. By 1903 the Black American workers appear to have been totally discouraged. Not only was there antagonism towards them in the community but their pay expectations had not been met and promises of good housing had not materialized.

As a group these men and their wives and children began, in the late summer of 1903, the long trek home.

Incredible as it must now seem, in the fall and winter of 1902-03 they began walking back to Alabama. First news of this appeared in *The Bangor Daily News* on 13 January, 1903. Wrote the *News*, "According to the story of Walter Griffin and his wife who applied at the police station here today for shelter for 250 coloured people who are walking home from Sydney C.B. to Alabama, a jaunt of about 2,900 miles. All are penniless, destitute and disappointed. The Griffins, who are scantily clad and suffered from hunger and cold, told a pitiful story." They had been promised, the newspaper said, good pay, and houses with gardens. They received very poor pay and there was frequent trouble with the mill owners who then brought in Italian workers from Pittsburgh. "The entire colony had decided to tramp back to Alabama and thought they could get there somehow and sometime." It was reported that many worked on farms along the way in order to survive. Some were ill and some died. How many got home is not now known.

CAPTAIN HORSFALL AND THE SCHOOL FOR SCANDAL

The early years of the twentieth century were ones of immense optimism in Canada. It was a time in which the country experienced phenomenal growth. Between 1901 and 1911 the population increased by 34%. Railway mileage doubled; wheat and lumber production increased tenfold. Mining production tripled. It has been estimated that between 1896 and 1914 three million immigrants entered Canada. Cape Breton shared the optimism. Mines expanded rapidly to meet the demands of the railways and the newly established steel plant in Sydney. But as farm workers sought the increased wages promised by industrial growth population declined in rural areas. Consequently the provincial government sought to encourage "intelligent, practical farmers who had some money of their own to come to the rural areas". Orphan children were shipped in from the Middlemore Home and Dr. Barnado's Homes in England to work on the farms.

One enterprising Sydney resident who had himself emigrated from England saw a flaw in the promotion efforts. Farmers needed not just cheap, child labour and money for equipment and land improvement. They needed women. Wives. Captain Frederick Horsfall. Royal Navy (ret) and his wife, Louise, from their home at Crawley's Creek, in Westmount across the harbour from Sydney, hatched a plan. In the early months of 1902 they advertised in the English press for "English girls of refinement" to come to their home for training that would enable them to grasp the opportunities offered in Canada. Mrs. Horsfall had "a long and varied experience in England, in teaching and training girls. She has traveled much in India, South Africa, Australia, the United States and Canada before settling here and can speak with authority on the needs of the Colonies for English teachers, housekeepers, lady-helps and wives."

The Horsfalls offered to receive into their home a number of "young gentlewomen" for a course of training of from one to three years. They would be thoroughly instructed in a wide range of topics including needlework, dressmaking, French, dairy work, poultry keeping and gardening. Extra topics included dancing, piano playing, German, Latin, typing and shorthand. All this was offered at what the *Sydney Record* was later to derisively call "Crawley Creek University" for forty guineas a year plus four guineas for each extra subject.

The English were used to scams and were as familiar with snake oil salesmen as Americans. Little attention may have been paid to the advertisement were it not for the endorsements. One was from the Bishop of Dover. Another came from a Mrs. Arnold-Forster who was said to be the sister-in-law of a prominent English official and the mother of a Lieutenant Arnold-Forster who had been in Canada recently on some work on behalf of the British government. As a result a number of young women decided to break away from the strictures of life in England and head for Cape Breton. One was a Miss Margaret

Hager, about twenty years old, former student at an English college for women and the daughter of Dr. Hager, a professor at Owen College, Manchester. She arrived in Sydney in November, 1902 and met there the first enrolled student, Miss Fanny Butterfield of Yorkshire. Shortly after the two girls were joined by others, including a Mrs. Egan and her daughters. Then Mrs. Arnold-Forster joined the ménage.

Throughout the remainder of November and into December life was fairly tranquil although, according to Miss Hager "there was never any attempt at carrying out the promises of the circular". Soon Mrs. Arnold-Forster returned to England and relationships at the "college" deteriorated rapidly. Miss Hager later reported that Captain Horsfall became verbally abusive, did no work himself and bullied his wife who, being sick most of the time, was unable to do any work at all and gave no instruction. The English girls' education consisted of doing the household chores, cleaning the poultry house and carrying water. They were given a bucksaw to cut firewood and their first lesson in farming was in attempting to plant strawberries in the snow.

Mrs. Horsfall prepared the following programs of study.

For Miss Hager:

7.30. Sweep and dust dining room. Lay breakfast. See that there is a good fire.

8.00. Breakfast. Remove breakfast.

9.00. Bedrooms to tidy and dust.

10.00. Lessons to noon.

12.00 – SEE THAT THERE IS A GOOD FIRE ALL DAY.

Clean dining room windows inside every Monday and Tuesday. Clean silver on other days. The dining room maid must keep dining room in perfect order, see lamp turned low when not in use and put out the lamp at 10.pm.

3.00.pm Do SOME out-door work, clean away snow, saw wood, etc.

4.00 pm. Needlework, dressmaking or repairing linen as needed.

5.30. Lay supper and remove supper.

To return me this paper at end of week and note every evening whether all the day's work has been punctually done.

If absent for any cause please that someone takes your place in the daily work, and inform me.

No one to be in the kitchen except while actually doing work, and work to be done quietly.

The tasks for Miss Butterfield were slightly different.

7.30. Hall and staircase to sweep.

8.30. Finish hall and staircase and dust. Keep hall and staircase tidy at all times.

ATTEND CAREFULLY TO THE HALL FIRE.

9.00. Bedroom to dust and tidy. Beds to make and floor to sweep

10.00. Brass stair rods, dining room and drawing room brasses to keep bright as her work every day.

11.00. Help Mrs. Egan to clean fowl house.

12.00. Saw wood for half hour when weather is suitable.

4.pm. Needlework.

Attend milking and learn how to do it.

See hall lamp out at 10. pm., and hall fire made up for night.

Return this paper at the end of the week. Note here every evening all the work been punctually and properly done. If absent for any cause please see that someone takes your place in the daily work and inform me. No one to be in the kitchen except when actually doing work, and work must be done quietly.

At first neighbours dropped by to socialize with the girls but that soon stopped since Captain Horsfall allegedly came home drunk and abusive. The girls were confined to their rooms and visits to Sydney were forbidden. Mrs. Egan, had soon had enough and told Horsfall she was going. The Captain demanded an extra quarter's rent and tuition. He approached a lawyer in order to begin action against Mrs. Egan and phoned the police demanding her forcible removal as "a disorderly woman". The girls meanwhile were confined to the upper story of the house where they lived off toast and tea while Mrs. Egan remained downstairs guarding all their belongings that, she feared, the Captain might otherwise steal.

At this point Margaret Hager showed leadership. She wrote a letter to the Reverend Woodroofe and to Sydney's Mayor Crowe which two of the other girls managed to smuggle out, then borrowed a sleigh from a neighbour and they all escaped to Sydney.

Thus Sydney's first attempt to have a college failed. The enraged Captain Horsfall initiated unsuccessful legal action for libel against the *Sydney Record* retaining J. A. Gillies K.C. and at the same time said that he had never thought much of the training plan but that it was really all his wife's idea. Furthermore, he said, Margaret Hager, who had said that the girls were all in a state of siege, was being hysterical. It was he that was in a state of siege and "had to lock myself in my room while they clamoured at the doors, beating them with their fists so that every moment I thought the locks would give."

The residents of Sydney were enraged. Letters flew to the *Sydney Record* and cartoons proliferated. Others, with tongues in cheek, regretted the outcry. Just when Cape Breton was trying to attract investment "the school established for the purpose of converting "verdant" English women into Colonial buck sawyers is pounced upon by the moral police force of Sydney and converted into a school for scandal."

>Wrote the *Sydney Record*,
>Alone upon the kitchen deck
>The gallant Captain stands;
>The lady tars have left the wreck,
>The ship is short of hands.
>
>He takes down his old telescope
>From the shelf above the door,
>And sweeps th' horizon full of hope;
>But no one sweeps the hen house floor.
>
>He dreams of those past pleasures now,
>When he ploughed the raging main;
>But now there's no one left to plow
>November's strawberry patch again.
>
>In those days when he watched the prow,
>As on the turret bridge he stood,
>He saw the chopping sea, but now
>
>Sees none to saw and chop the wood.

ROBERT J. PEARY - NORTHWARD HO!

Sydney Harbour, as most people know well, has long been important in the early exploration of the northern part of the continent. It was, and continues to be the closest rail-connected port in North America to Europe and continues in importance even to today when cruise liners make more of an impact on public awareness. What few know is its past significance in polar exploration. For, not so long past, it was the step off point for some aiming at the North Pole. Perhaps because of the greater availability of supplies, partly because of its communication facility, and particularly the ready availability coal, it even surpassed for some St. John's, Newfoundland; certainly this was true for the expedition that finally reached the Pole.

There had been earlier northern-bound expeditions with a Cape Breton connection. One, which set off in 1881, sponsored by the American army, contained Cape Bretoner George Rice, a photographer from North Sydney who had been given the honorary rank of sergeant by rank-conscious Adolphus W. Greely. The expedition was not a happy one. The Greely expedition anchored itself at the northern end of Ellesmere Island, way north of Baffin Land, at a base they called Fort Conger. From there they made stabs towards the North Pole. Relief supplies failed to reach them and in the late summer of 1883 the expedition began the trudge south, hoping to meet a relief ship on its way. They did not. As they progressed the bickering, always present, escalated and even mutiny – it was a military expedition – became a possibility.

The one person whom the others appeared to respect and who was described as "the hero of the journey" was George Rice. Soon, having for weeks drifted on an ice flow and now close to starvation, Rice headed out on foot to seek for possible food caches. He found some, enough food for only a couple of months. Rice's behavior throughout the ill-fated expedition appears to have been exemplary. Regrettably, little more is known of his repeated and courageous acts than the surviving notes of his companions. Rice, a hero long forgotten, died struggling to find food for the others. The survivors were eventually rescued, six men, including Greely, of an original party of twenty-five.

The United States greeted news of the discovery of the survivors ecstatically. Thousands poured out to meet the relief ship at Portsmouth, and it was only later, when horrifying aspects of the expedition became known, that questions as to the advisability of arctic exploration were raised.

When the survivors of Greely's expedition reached home Robert E. Peary was a young lieutenant in the United States navy. Despite the welter of melancholy information, including cannibalism among Greely's survivors, young Peary's hopes were focused on the north.

It was perhaps memories of Greely and the courageous Rice that prompted acerbic comment in the *North Sydney Herald* on 19 July, 1893, when Peary was stabbing for the Pole.

> The enterprise and determination which have characterized Lieut Peary in undertaking another Arctic voyage, commands our admiration but it is impossible to approve his judgment. It is hardly within the range of possibilities that he will be able to carry out his design of reaching the north pole by an overland trip and planting the stars and stripes thereon. But even if he should, of what service will the exploit be to humanity? It will not render the trip any easier for others to take or to this furnish any good or sufficient reason why they should take it if it is easier. There is not the slightest probability that trade will be opened up with the extreme north or that any real good will come to science, to art or to industry from any results which Lieut Peary may secure. Being so, the expedition is a foolhardy one and no amount of courage or daring or enthusiasm on the part of that explorer or his estimable wife can prevent its being so regarded by those who look plain facts in the face.

In 1887 Peary's vessel, the *Hope* arrived at North Sydney bound for Baffin Land. The ship bunkered coal at New Cambellton and among those who were registered at the Vendome Hotel were Captain Jay Jensen who was on his way to take charge of a whaling station on Baffin Island, students of the Massachusetts Institute of Technology who were to collect etymological specimens for New York and Chicago museums, geological explorers and a hunting party. "They serenaded a party of French ladies who were spending a summer at the Vendome Hotel".

Lieutenant Peary had made his first trip to the north reconnoitering the Greenland ice cap. In 1891 he traveled one thousand three hundred miles by sled across Greenland He was accompanied by his wife who became the first white woman to be part of an Arctic expedition. In 1893 Peary was again accompanied by his wife who gave birth to a daughter during the expedition. In 1894 Peary discovered three large meteorites that had been used by the Eskimos to make iron implements and on his return brought the two smaller ones with him. In 1898, when he inspired the above comment, he was about to make his first effort to reach the Pole. In December of that same year he got as far as Fort Conger, Greely's base camp. Undeterred he tried for the Pole again in 1900. In 1901, when nothing had been heard from him after his departure in 1900, Mrs. Peary stopped in Sydney with a relief party. When she found him safe at Etah, in Greenland she returned with a shipload of walrus heads and kayak souvenirs.

In 1903, following a behind-the-scenes struggle with Adolphus Greely, he became president of the American Geographical Society. But he wanted the Pole. Despite the wishes of his wife and daughter, he remained determined to push north again. He raised money to construct a purpose-built ship, the *Roosevelt*, determined that his companions would live in snow houses – reusable on the return journey – and would dress in native clothing. They once again gathered their stores and coal in North Sydney and Sydney before continuing on. Commanding his ship was thirty-six year old Captain Robert Bartlett of Newfoundland. Among those who accompanied him was his black assistant, Matthew Henson. Bartlett rammed the *Roosevelt* through the pack ice as far as possible, then Henson and a group of Eskimos headed the land party further north. Peary, Henson and their group of Eskimos did not reach the Pole, but they did get closer than anyone else had and wrote a book <u>Nearest the Pole</u> to compensate for his disappointment.

Another hero of this attempt was the captain of the *Roosevelt*. Bob Bartlett demonstrated incredible skill and tenacity bring his ship back home to New York. About the time that Peary was boarding a train in Sydney to head south Bartlett's ship had run aground trying to pass through the locks at St. Peter's Canal without a rudder. Christmas Eve, 1906, the Roosevelt reached New York Harbor and was soon being prepared for yet another attempt.

The tenacious Peary, now a naval Commander, tried once more. On 17 July, 1908, he and his companions again sailed out of Sydney Harbour bound for the Pole as he had done so many times before. He bought and loaded most of his supplies at Vooght's Wharf in North Sydney and the ships bunkered with coal while there. Then they sailed again for Etah in Greenland. With one hundred thirty three dogs and nineteen sledges, five white men and his indispensable black assistant, Matt Henson, and seven Eskimos he pushed on through the winter. On 6 April, 1909, Peary, Henson and four of the Eskimos reached the Pole.

On 21 September Peary and his party aboard the *SS Roosevelt* reached Sydney. News of their achievement had been cabled ahead from Etah two weeks earlier and an enormous flotilla of crafts of every description greeted him as he sailed into Sydney Harbour. Thousands awaited his arrival. "At 9 am crowds began climbing on steamers, yachts, motor boats, rowboats and canoes. At 9.30 the schools closed and students flocked to the waterfront. Every tram from the mining towns came in crowded". In the center of the harbour the *Tam o'*

Shanter was packed with flower girls. Earlier that morning the yacht *Sheelah*, owned by Mr. Ross, a senior executive at the steel plant, set off with Mrs. Peary and her two children. They intercepted the *SS Roosevelt* at 7.30 and a gig carried them across for an emotional reunion with the commander.

As the *Roosevelt* approached it was greeted by the Sydney fleet of welcome off Cranberry Head. As the armada sailed towards the docks at Sydney there was "perfect pandemonium and screaming whistles as the parade of ships steamed up the harbour". On the opposite shore it was estimated that practically the entire population of North Sydney – whose people had a special warmth for the Peary explorers since so much of their earlier efforts had focused on the town – turned out to watch, wave and cheer. From the mizzen gaff of the *Roosevelt* flew a large Stars and Stripes across which, on both sides Henson had sewn a white diagonal strip emblazoned with the words NORTH POLE.

Coming ashore the explorer and his family went to the Sydney Hotel for a civic reception. Said Mayor Richardson, "Next to a Canadian or a citizen of our mother country no man can or should receive from us a heartier welcome".

Once home, Peary wrote to the American consul stationed in Sydney, for onward transmission to the mayor and people of the city, "I cannot say how deeply I have been gratified by the splendid welcome given me by the City of Sydney. There is a very tender spot in my heart for Sydney; eleven different summers have I gone north from here, returning with various measures of success, until at last I have won that to which I have devoted the best years of my life. Here I have repeatedly said goodbye to those who are near and dear to me, and here they have greeted me upon my return. The generous ovation given seems a fitting climax to a series of memories, which I shall always carry with me. PEARY."

In 1911 Peary retired from the Navy with the rank of rear-admiral. He wrote books but was troubled by debate over the veracity of his claim to have been first to the Pole.

Recognition for Matt Henson came later. In 1913 President Taft arranged for him to become a clerk in the New York Customs House where he stayed until 1936. During that decade he earned a master's degree from Harvard University and in 1944 received the Congressional Medal of Honor. Shortly before he died on 5 March, 1955 in New York City he was received at the White House by President Eisenhower. There was to be a happy, albeit tardy sequel. Research by a Harvard professor during the later years of the twentieth century discovered that while in the north both Peary and Henson had sons by Eskimo women. The Peary and Henson Eskimo descendents traveled to the United States to be present when the body of Matthew Henson was re-interred alongside that of Peary in Arlington National Cemetery. In November, 2000 Henson was posthumously awarded the National Geographic Society's Hubbard Medal.

Captain Bartlett, captain of the *Roosevelt*, went on to further his international reputation as a brilliant sailor and navigator and continued to take scientists, photographers and students to the north. In 1913-14 he commanded the *Karluk* on Stefansson's Canadian government Arctic expedition. Like Peary and Hansen he was awarded the Hubbard medal. In 1946 he contracted pneumonia and died in a New York hospital. He never married and had no children. He is buried in Brigus, Newfoundland and today his home is a Canadian National Heritage site.

Had he lived the author of that snippy article in the *North Sydney Herald* might have revised some views. Shortly after Peary and Henson's success it became more widely accepted that adoption of native clothing and equipment increased the chances of survival. He proved that Greenland was an island and he improved the quality of pemmican. More than anything he demonstrated the virtue of sheer tenacity in pursuing the need of humans to seek out and conquer new frontiers.

"THOSE DARING MEN AND THEIR FLYING MACHINES"

In the early afternoon of 23 February, 1909, bitterly cold but warmly remembered by the crowds that watched, the *Silver Dart*, brainchild of Alexander Graham Bell and his co-workers, lifted off the ice of the Bras d'Or near Baddeck. Piloted by Canadian, and local Baddecker, J.A.D. McCurdy, it became the first plane to fly in the British Empire. Its success was a result of the combined endeavors of a British, American, and Canadian team working together in the Aircraft Experimental Association; four daring young men and one old genius.

Our memory of early flying has been coloured and distorted by those sepia prints of Victorian figures ascending in their balloons. Top hatted, frock coated, gaily loosening the rope that secures their wicker basket compartments to the ground at the Paris Exposition or the Crystal Palace, their images are far more indelible than those of the great dirigibles that flew early in the last century. *"Around the World in Eighty Days"* was, as we imagined, far more fun than the reality.

They Came From Away

For those early pioneers the reality could be grim. In 1875, for example, three men went up in their balloon called the *Zenith* and reached a height of almost twenty eight thousand feet. Only one man survived. The other two died from lack of oxygen. At much the same time as the Wright brothers were experimenting with their flying machine two Germans floated up from Berlin to nearly thirty-five thousand feet – about the altitude of current trans-Atlantic jumbo-jets.

Those early entrepreneurs needed more than inventiveness; they need raw courage. As the need for courage receded the need for science grew. One man who experimented with balloons, not with a view of using them to go aloft, but to understand air currents, was the scientist Alexander Graham Bell. Bell was already renowned as the inventor of the telephone and though less well known for his efforts using electronic to find the bullet in the body of President Garfield before he succumbed to assassination, he epitomized the energetic inventiveness of the nineteenth century. When only eleven years old he invented a device to clean the husks off grains of wheat. Throughout his life he investigated an array of challenges from hearing aids to the productivity of sheep. Now his attention focused on the air. His headquarters was his house, Beinn Bhreagh near Baddeck.

Alexander Graham Bell was born in Edinburgh, Scotland in 1847 of a distinguished scientific family and came with his father, to Canada when he was twenty- three. Soon after this they moved to the United States. Bell and his wife Mabel, after years of sailing the Atlantic seaboard, decided in 1885, that even though it was a long way from Washington D.C. they, like so many others who followed them, would make their summer home near Baddeck. Though not the first they were without any doubt the most distinguished "from awayers".

Kites, and what could be learned from them, fascinated Bell. To overcome the problem presented by increasing the weight without correspondingly increasing the lift he joined a number of kites together and produced the tetrahedral kite, a four-sided, lightweight aluminum frame covered with silk. One, the *Frost King*, lifted thirty feet into the air and supported a 165 lb man hanging from a rope.

Dr. Bell had been trying to solve the mystery of flight as early as 1891 when experimenting with propellers and, in an article he wrote at this time called *"Flying Machines of the Future"*, envisaged airplanes capable of carrying passengers over long distances. Many years of experimenting with kites to understand aerodynamics were beginning to reap rewards.

It was as a result of the success of the experiment with kites that Bell formed the Aerial Experiment Association in October of 1907 and less than a year and a half later their *Silver Dart* lifted off the ice to fly using the first air-cooled aircraft engine. The success resulted from the combined efforts of a small group: Bell's tenacious pursuit of his goal, his wife's willingness to put up the initial capital, $20,000 of her own money, to fund the Association, and four young men. One was a U.S. Army lieutenant, Thomas Selfridge. Casey Baldwin was Chief Engineer and J.A.D. McCurdy was Treasurer. Glen Curtiss was Director of Experiments.

Frederick Walker "Casey" Baldwin was an engineer and recent graduate of the University of Toronto. The other Canadian was a fellow student, J.A.D. McCurdy from Baddeck. The two "awayers" were Lieutenant Thomas E. Selfridge and Glenn Curtiss.

Tom Selfridge graduated from the West Point Military Academy and entered the artillery. His first interest was flying and he tried to join the Wright brothers but they turned him down. Then he met Bell who was so impressed with him that he made a direct appeal to President Theodore Roosevelt to have Selfridge assigned as an official military observer and thus Selfridge became a member of the A.E.A. on indefinite leave.

Bell met Curtiss at a motor show in New York soon after the then twenty-four year old had opened a plant making motorcycle engines. Curtiss was rapidly making a reputation for himself and built the engine for the California Arrow, an early dirigible. His factory at Hammondsport, New York, was already employing eighty-five men when, in 1907, in response to Bell's suggestion, he headed to Cape Breton to participate in the exciting new venture. The first craft was the *Cygnet*, a giant tetrahedral kite with Selfridge on board. But a kite was not the ultimate aim. They needed a small engine that could power a plane. That's where Curtiss was needed and he built a 40-horsepower, 8-cylinder gasoline engine. Four planes were designed, the *Red Wing*, named because of the red silk that covered its wings, the *White Wing*, the *June Bug*, and the *Silver Dart*. They were tried out back at Curtiss' plant at Hammondsport where crash followed crash.

Success came in Hammondsport with the first public airplane flight in the United States (the Wright brother flights had not been public). Then the *White Wing* flew with a tricycle undercarriage for take-off and landing and incorporating the ailerons, which allowed directional control of the plane and were designed by Curtiss. Next, Glenn Curtiss flew the *June Bug*. This flight won the coveted Scientific American Prize for the first airplane flight in the United States of more than one kilometer.

Bell was eager to have one of their machines flown in Canada. On 23 February, 1909, a bitterly cold day, with J.A.D. McCurdy at the controls, the *Silver Dart* lifted off from the ice of the Bras d'Or Lakes. This was the first heavier than air powered flight in Canada and the British Empire and it might not have happened if Canadian Customs' wish to prevent the *Silver Dart* from entering the country had not been overturned. Following an urgent request from Baddeck they allowed it to enter duty-free provided that it did not stay in Canada for more than two years. Wrote McCurdy later, "And so on that day Feb 23 1909, was introduced to the Empire not only an epoch-making flight, but the three-wheel or tricycle undercarriage and the aileron itself – without which maneuverability, both in war and civilian aircraft – would be impossible. I consider these two inventions possibly Canada's greatest contributions to world-wide aviation."

The success had not been without setback. There were numerous crashes and some injuries. Tragedy as well. Lieutenant Selfridge, who flew for the first time on Baldwin-designed *White Wing*, was assigned to Fort Myers, Virginia. On 17 September, 1908, on a test flight with Orville Wright, their engine exploded and the plane crashed. Wright, though injured survived. Selfridge died. The crash had occurred fifty yards from the gate of Arlington National Cemetery, and it was here that he was buried with full military honours.

All had placed their names in the history books. Selfridge is memorialized in United States Air Force institutions. Casey Baldwin became a distinguished Canadian airman and developed with Bell a hydrofoil that, in 1919 became, traveling at seventy-one mile per-hour the fastest ship in the world. He died at the age of sixty-six at his home near Baddeck. With Mabel's encouragement he had come to Baddeck for a few months. He stayed for forty years. J.A.D.McCurdy later became Nova Scotia's Lieutenant Governor. Before that he barnstormed across America, was a stunt flyer and racer and demonstrated the value of bombing from the air. He tried to convince Ottawa of the strategic value of aircraft but government officials ridiculed the airplane as "the invention of the devil". Ironically, the Canadian government, in the Second World War asked McCurdy to become director of government aircraft production. In the summer of 2009, marking the one hundredth anniversary of the flight of the *Silver Dart*, the Sydney Airport was renamed J.A.D. McCurdy Airport in his honour.

Glenn Curtiss went on to make successful seaplanes and was involved in the development of aircraft carriers, but his greatest contribution to flying was the invention, in his early A.E.A. days, of the aileron. He created the first American aircraft factory. In 1917 his factories produced thousands of military training planes for Britain, Russia and the United States and the first practical seaplanes. One of his Navy-Curtiss planes, the NC-4 Thin 1919 made the first trans-Atlantic flight. He died in Buffalo, New York in 1930.

Alexander Graham Bell is largely remembered today for his invention of the telephone, but there was much, much more as a visit to the Bell Museum in Baddeck vividly illustrates. He died on Cape Breton on 2 August, 1922. At the moment of his burial all telephone service throughout the United States was halted for one minute in tribute to this remarkable man.

Mabel died five months later. Her generous donation for the creation of the Aerial Experiment Association had triggered their successes. The A.E.A. was dissolved after eighteen months. It had accomplished its objective to put a man in the air.

JACK HOLMES - HANGMAN

This is a macabre story, not one for the squeamish. While murder had been rare on Cape Breton until the Second World War and there had been none between 1833 and 1913, it is odd that all those executed had "come from away" as had their hangmen.

Today no one knows what attracted Jack Holmes to Canada; was it ambition or fear? Whatever the cause, in 1915 he was leaving on the train from Sydney to Halifax for the third time in a year.

Holmes' early career as hangman was in the United States. He was not a large man, just 5' 8" and slightly built, but he was ambitious. In 1906 he had become the official hangman in the State of Georgia and he had obtained fame – or notoriety – for his execution of a minister, the Reverend Turner who had been found guilty of inciting a racial riot in Jackson, Florida. It was an execution that may have buttressed an inflated ego because it became a theatrical event attracting a large crowd. In those days in parts of the southern United States executions were held in the open and anyone who wanted to attend could. On the day slated for the event it was raining hard and so that Turner's relatives could watch the event in comfort Holmes commandeered a large theatre and Turner died before a sellout audience.

By the time Holmes headed north into Canada he had, or so he told a reporter, executed twenty Americans; eight in Georgia, five in Tennessee, four in Alabama and three in Arkansas. In Canada he settled initially in Regina and it may have been that since the old spirit of the lawless American West was dying and Canada was seeing waves of new immigration he thought there was more opportunity here.

Added to that, Canada's principal hangman was, perhaps almost literally falling down on the job. John Robert Radclive's reputation had declined since a double execution had gone badly in Montreal in 1899. A rural church organist, Cordelia Viau and her lover, Sam Parslow were hanged for murdering Cordelia's husband. But the event got out of hand. The hanging of a woman was a popular event but despite Radclive's attempts to limit the sale of tickets to two hundred, outside a mob of two thousand – men, women and children – clamored for admission. The mob attacked the prison doors, shots were fired over their heads to keep them at bay, while inside the ticket holders, by now thoroughly excited, tore down the curtains surrounding the gallows. Adding to the stress of the day the death of neither of the prisoners had been instant. Radclive hurried back to his room and drank a bottle of brandy.

Radclive, like Holmes had "come from away" He had learned his trade in the Royal Navy on pirates in the South China Sea. On leaving the navy he apprenticed himself to the Lincolnshire hangman William Marwood who, incidentally executed the murderer of David's Great-Great Grandfather, John Newton. After immigrating to Canada he first settle in Toronto and after passing his CV to various sheriffs again became a hangman. Although widely used, he botched a number of executions and became known for such sleazy sidelines as selling the clothes of his victims and hawking the rope used for a dollar an inch. His successor later remarked that as many as three ropes were sold after a single execution. Then, on another occasion the condemned man collapsed and died in his arms before he pulled the lever. It was all too much and Radclive's drinking became obsessive. Jack Holmes may have seen this as his opportunity.

Radclive died in Toronto in 1912 and the post became open. Holmes was to be disappointed again. Another immigrant, Arthur English, had the right credentials. He had served widely in the British Army and retired with the rank of captain. He had relatives in the hanging trade and they taught him some of the ropes, as it were. He immigrated to Canada, settled in Montreal, changed his name to Arthur Ellis, becoming official hangman in 1913 and Canada's most renowned executioner until his retirement in 1935.

There was still plenty of work for Holmes as Ellis was not always available. Though Holmes had hanged others, in May 1914, he made his first trip to Sydney to hang an American, Frank Haynes.

Haynes was a confidence man and drifter on the run for bigamy and a variety of charges from Arizona to California. He was wanted for forgery in Flagstaff, and in the words of the Sheriff of Coconino County he was "the smoothest character ever to enter Arizona". During his travels in the west he may have met Tena Atkinson, the wife of Sydney hotelier Ben Atkinson, in Los Angeles or San Francisco and almost certainly did in Winnipeg. Later he saw her in New Glasgow, Nova Scotia before coming to Cape Breton. Haynes was popular in the watering holes of Sydney. He could spin a good yarn and shoot expansive lines about his exploits. He was what Texans might have called "all hat and no cattle". He specialized, he said, in minerals, mining schemes and women.

In August Tena's husband, Ben Atkinson, owner of the Minto Hotel on Charlotte Street, was killed near the family's summer campsite on Front Lake Road. Haynes was charged with murder. Later Tena and her uncle were also charged in the case. The trial aroused intense public interest because of the social prominence of many associated with the family and the local conviction that Tena had plotted with Haynes.

After Haynes was found guilty the appeal process was most irregular. Since the evidence was largely circumstantial, there was hope that the death sentence would be commuted, as it had been in half the cases in the last decade, and Jim Maddin, his defense lawyer was in Ottawa to pursue this appeal. But with death imminent Haynes confessed – and not to his own lawyer who was in Ottawa but to the prosecutor. Some years later the story emerged of what actually happened when Maddin was in Ottawa seemingly fighting for Haynes' life. The Canadian Justice Minister called a meeting to consider commutation. They had apparently just about decided on it when the telegram arrived with Haynes' confession. "Has he implicated anyone" asked Maddin. "Yes, Mrs Atkinson". Tena Atkinson was Jim Maddin's aunt. "Let's go see a movie" said Maddin, and that was the end of it.

There was near rioting on the streets and when Holmes arrived to carry out the sentence he botched it. He had misjudged Haynes weight believing him lighter than he was and the victim was almost decapitated.

The next execution to bring Holmes back to Sydney was in November, 1914. This was another botched execution and of another "from awayer". A Polish immigrant, Gustav Brauer raped and murdered a small girl. There was local horror at the crime but it stimulated far less newspaper interest because the Great War had begun and was dominating the news Bauer, initially described as Polish was now referred to as German, reflecting or contributing to the anti-German sentiments now sweeping the country. Again Holmes misjudged his victim's weight, lighter than Holmes thought and Bauer was strangled over several minutes.

Holmes was more successful on his next visit. This man, a forty-seven year old black man named John West raped and murdered a seventy year old spinster Carrie Dunn at her home on Queen Street in North Sydney. Holmes must have feared that, like the previous two it would prove difficult. It did not. West walked to the gallows with composure and with other prisoners singing "Nearer My God to Thee". Before the black hood was adjusted over his head he smiled at Captain Galloway of the Salvation Army, pulled himself to his full height and stepped onto the trap. He died instantly. He had shown courage earlier. When he and two others were held for a couple of weeks for questioning as suspects, in order to spare the other two West confessed. West said "he did not want to see the other two blamed for what he had done." The murder trial was the shortest in Nova Scotia's modern history with few, other than Captain Galloway and the Reverend Raynor present. The press was not interested. The war in Europe buried the news of the execution in the middle pages.

When Holmes left Sydney bound for Halifax he must have wondered if he would ever be back again. Many years passed before he did come back and unlike the almost unnoticed earlier hanging this, the last one on the island, far from being ignored almost caused an international incident. Again, the hanged man was a "from awayer", an American.

Invalgd "Bing" Anderson was from Berlin, New Hampshire. He arrived in Sydney in the last week of January 1930, and described himself as a bond salesman when registering in the Norfolk Hotel under the name of Emmett Sloane. It was said he had been an internationally known ski jumper but had become something of a drifter. He claimed to have served overseas in the Great War, spent time in Montreal and took up selling bonds when he came to Halifax. He had something of a record and had served time for jumping trains.

On the night of 8 February, 1930 Sloane, as he was most widely known, beat to death Debois Rehburg, the night clerk at the hotel. It was conjectured that Sloane wanted to rob the hotel's safe but no money had been taken and Reburg was found on the blood-spattered bed in Sloane's room.

Following the killing Sloane headed out of Sydney on foot to the nearby community of Ball's Creek. On Monday, two days following the killing CJCB Radio broadcast a description of him and a Mrs. Campbell who lived on Campbell's Hill near Ball's Creek, remembered seeing him. She phoned the police. Over the weekend there had been heavy snow and two policemen had to use a horse to break a road through to Ball's Creek where they found Sloane using the name Brown signed on at a lumber camp. The cook at the camp had also heard the radio description and was able to point out "Brown" to the police.

Sloane was tried in March, confessed the killing and was sentenced to die.

Jack Holmes nearly missed the execution. The official hangman, Arthur Ellis had been expected to do the job but another execution, in Chatham, Ontario took precedence and Holmes was appointed. The execution caused debate and controversy on two counts. Out west a

Herman Revinski was due to be executed at the end of February for murdering a Toronto bond salesman, David Katz. Revinski strongly denied committing the crime suggesting that Sloane may have done it. This execution was postponed until 11 March when it was carried out.

The principal reason surrounding the controversy over Sloane's sentence was his mental state. Dr. Claire of Guelph, Ontario was the only psychiatrist – or alienist as they were then called – allowed to examine him. Claire declared him sane. American authorities, reported to have been the State or War Department in Washington D.C. and the government of New Hampshire, wanted another alienist, Dr. John Marshal of Halifax to examine Sloane but this was refused. Considerable bitterness was expressed in the United States where many thought that Sloane (Anderson) was insane "and had been for years".

Alfred Halverson, said to have been a relative of Sloane, came to Sydney from Berlin, New Hampshire, to add his plea. Said Halverson, Sloane "had great ability as a ski jumper." He was selected in 1925 to go to Europe to represent the Eastern Ski Jumpers Association but officials had withdrawn his name because of his strange actions and attitudes. "In 1926 we expelled him from the ski club because of his irresponsible tendencies." Added Halverson, "It was on grounds of his irresponsibility that his wife secured a divorce."

Despite vocal condemnation in the United States of Canadian justice and the claims that he was insane, he was hanged and buried in Hardwood Hill cemetery alongside Frank Haynes, Gustav Brauer and John West. Sloane was not the last person to die on Cape Breton in this way.

On 30 April, 1931 forty-two year old George Beckett from Old Pelican, Newfoundland was hanged for the murder of Glace Bay taxi driver Nicolas Marthos. Until the day before it was thought that Holmes would again officiate. This did not happen. At the last the official hangman from Quebec arrived. The reason for Holmes displacement is not now known.

Another man came perilously close to dying in this way. Walter Wilkinson of Table Head was sentenced to die for the murder in 1933 of his sister-in-law English war bride Winnifred Wilkinson. Just prior to his hanging his defense attorney, Jim Maddin won his argument that there had been a mistrial. A second trial acquitted Wilkinson.

There have been no execution on Cape Breton since that of Beckett although sadly there have been more murders. It is also of interest that of all those hanged on Cape Breton since its earliest days have, apart from resident Mrs. Flahaven in 1833, "come from away".

While Marthos' killer was the last hanged on the island death for convicted murderers continued in Canada until 1962 when two men died for killing police officers. After that capital punishment was finally abolished in Canada.

"GUS' EDWARDS – COAL MINER TO AIR MARSHAL

When Harold Edwards came to Canada from England in 1903 he was only eleven years old. Nevertheless, he would remember for years to come the small town of Chorley in Lancashire that had been his home and have recognized the enormous difference between that town and New Aberdeen, his new home.

Chorley then was as large as Sydney today and larger than Glace Bay where Edwards' father worked as an electrician. Their new home was adjacent to Glace Bay, in the community of New Aberdeen and the entire area was dominated, as it had been for decades, by the coal industry. The Dominion Coal Company, formed in 1893, was the focus of all activity in the area. It was said "either you are a servant of the coal company or the servant of a servant of the company". Other opportunities were negligible. Glace Bay was a company town – the town's first mayor was also general superintendent of the company stores.

When the Edwards family arrived the new coalmine, Number 2 Colliery, had only been open five years and New Aberdeen had grown up around it. Harold Edwards would have been aware of the raw newness of his surroundings that compared unfavorably with those he had just left. Wooden shacks, open sewers, newly constructed clapboard houses were harsh contrasts to the red brick and proudly polished front steps of workers' homes in Lancashire and there were nowhere nearby the ancient churches or the affluent homes of the richer residents of Lancashire. To the eleven-year old Harold – nicknamed "Gus" after a popular music hall comedian of the times – that would not have mattered. What he had left was more than compensated for by the sense of opportunity and an adventure. His mother may have been more aware of what she had left behind and his father, having electrical skills, probably had a higher wage than most in the community.

Then in 1906 tragedy struck. Edwards, senior, was killed in an industrial accident and the now fourteen-year old "Gus" had to go to work. In New Aberdeen in the early years of the twentieth century, that meant working "in the pit". During this period Dominion Coal, which had been founded by Henry Melville Whitney – who also owned Dominion Iron and Steel in Sydney – had fallen under the control of Montreal and Toronto financiers. The colliery doctor, A.S. Kendall summed up the two leading management figures. "J. H. Plummer – an Englishman stubborn and cruel out of time and out of place in Canada even at that date. James Ross was a rich savage who arrived in Canada well equipped as an engineer but insensitive to the needs of humanity."

Glace Bay was fraught with tension. On 8 July, 1909 more than five hundred officers and men of the Canadian Army moved by train from Halifax to Glace Bay ostensibly to protect the collieries from strikers.

Decades of friction between management and the miners of Glace Bay would follow and young Edwards was at the centre. What his roll was, if any, is unknown, but there can be little doubt that when war with Germany began many, including Edwards, saw an opportunity to escape the grim confrontations within the town.

Work in the pit ended for good for Gus Edwards in the late summer of 1914. He immediately joined the merchant marine where, as an able bodied seaman he was paid eighty-five cents a day. With the outbreak of war Ottawa's interest in aviation was accelerating. The War Office in London expressed an interest in recruiting British-born pilots in North America but, as was soon discovered, there were all too few of them. By the spring of 1915 only five had been recruited and sent to England. The Royal Naval Air Service was also trying to recruit in Canada and it too ran into the same problem. Too few trained airmen. Consequently they established a private flying school near Toronto where embryonic flyers could train and acquire the necessary certificates of competence. The man responsible was J.A.D. McCurdy who was at that time with the Curtiss Aeroplane Company at Hammondsport in New York. In mid-April, 1915 McCurdy advertised in newspapers in Canada for recruits who would be accepted as pilots in the RNAS once they had their flying licenses. The Curtiss School charged each would-be pilot $400 but volunteers could have part of their costs recovered by a gratuity once they qualified. The response was immediate. In June, 1915, Able Seaman Gus Edwards joined the volunteers and although he had little formal training or education, was accepted.

A problem for many of the volunteers was that they simply could not afford extended and expensive training. A compromise solution to the problem emerged. "A special company of the Royal Naval Canadian Volunteer Reserve was formed and the RNAS candidates were invited to join it. Eighteen did so and were given transportation to Halifax where they boarded *HMCS Niobe* as able seamen in the RNCVR." Gus Edwards was one of the eighteen. It was on *HMCS Niobe* that Edwards and the other recruits had their basic naval training before appointment as probationary flight sub-lieutenants and being shipped to Europe.

In August, 1916, Edwards was posted to #3 Naval Bombing Wing and stationed at Luxiel-les-Bains, on the Western Front about sixty miles west of the German city of Freiburg. The Wing came under the control of the British Admiralty that at that time strongly favoured retaliation against Germany that had used its huge airships for bombing raids on civilian centers in England. The British air force had little defense against these "zeppelins" so named after their inventor. What little defense they had, dropping darts on them from above, had proved ineffective. So retaliation against German cities was favoured though the authorities hesitated to use it. Attitudes changed. A raid on the English city of Hull set off rioting among the population and the mobbing of a Royal Flying Corps officer. After that the British complained of other atrocities. Nurse Edith Cavell was executed. Passenger ships the *Lusitania* and *Sussex* were sunk.

Neglected allied prisoners of war were dying of typhoid. A merchant marine captain who attempted to ram a U-boat attacking him was executed on the grounds that he had contravened the rules of war. Passions were boiling and the public cried out for a captured German naval officer to be executed in return. This could not be countenanced, but when the Germans sank the hospital ship *Asturias* public opinion demanded revenge. The British government decided to use #3 Wing to attack the city of Freiburg. The attack did not go well but a subsequent attack composed entirely of Canadians and including Edwards and the soon to be famous Raymond Collishaw, was more successful. But Edwards was shot down and made a prisoner of war. The jubilation at the success of the reprisal raid was offset in Britain by the news that a major section of Freiburg University had been destroyed and the sentiment was expressed in Parliament that the government did not wish to compete with the enemy over reprisals.

The surviving pilots of the Luxiel Wing were transferred to the Royal Flying Corps, their Sopwith Camels were given to the French and Gus Edwards remained in a prison camp until the end of the war. As he laconically noted in his entry in <u>Who's Who</u> he acquired much of his education studying in Germany.

What would come next? That question perplexed Edwards and when he met Collishaw in London the answer was soon forthcoming. There was a need for airmen in Russia. The Bolshevik Revolution overtook Russia in 1917 and, under Lenin Russia, which had suffered horrendous casualties in the war, signed a separate peace. Soon the entire country was embroiled in civil war. Lenin's withdrawal of Russia from war had enabled tens of thousands of German troops to be transferred from the eastern front to the western and in the spring of 1918 the re-invigorated German Army looked as if it might soon be victorious. Only the halting of their spring offensive and the arrival of American forces proved to the German generals that in the long run they could not succeed. Germany surrendered. But a residual effect of Lenin's separate peace was to encourage the western allies to intervene, initially to keep the eastern front open, in Russia's civil war between Reds and Whites in favour of the anti-communists, the Whites. The Canadian government saw no reason for involvement but Canadian airmen by this time were scattered throughout the Royal Air Force and thus subject to British jurisdiction.

A group of flyers, led by Collishaw and including Gus Edwards composed 47 Squadron whose task it was to be part of an RAF instructional mission to train White Russians under General Deniken to fly. Collishaw's 47 Squadron was composed of three flights of single-seated Sopwith Camels and three flights of de Haviland 9 bombers. Their campaigning was unlike anything experienced on the relatively static Western Front. The squadron acted as air support for three of Denikin's White Russian armies. These were the Kuban Cossacks operating out of Tsaritsyn, (later named Stalingrad and still later Volgograd), the Don Cossacks and the Volunteer Army of the Ukraine. They fought Red pilots who included in their number demobilized German pilots and they strafed Red Army cavalry units. The Canadian flyers traveled like nomads, their planes on railroad flatcars following the armies. Reds and Whites fought each other with incredible savagery and had any Canadian pilots been captured his death would have been inevitable and slow.

Although there were times when it seemed that the White armies would win – Denikin's forces pushed north to within a few hundred miles of Moscow – White disunity and incompetence and the electrifying effect of Trotsky's organization of the Red Army soon turned Denikin's troops into a retreating mob.

Edwards was with "C" Flight of 47 Squadron that became separated from Collishaw's main body. Collishaw was all but cut off in the Caucasus during the collapse of the White army, and had to fight its way out of encirclement towards the Black Sea. Eventually traveling by armoured train and encumbered with refugees and their baggage, they reached their goal of the Crimea and evacuation.

Edwards, with "C" Flight was attached to the Kuban Cossacks. They struggled through the Caucasus Mountains and finally reached Novorossisk on the eastern shore of the Black Sea. As the Red Army closed in stores were bulldozed into the sea, panic spread and some Whites committed suicide rather than be captured by the Reds. "C" Flight and the remnants of Denikin's army managed to reach British warships offshore and were carried to the Crimea to battle on. It was a battle that did not last long. Collishaw and Edwards, together again in 47 Squadron continued flying in support of the Crimean White army but in the late spring of 1920 the British Military Mission was withdrawn. For his activities the White Russians awarded Edwards the Order of St. Stanislaus and the Order of Ste. Anne.

Back again in London Edwards again faced the problem of what to do next. Like many other Canadian flyers who participated in anti-Bolshevik crusade, Edwards was probably not motivated by any philosophical commitment. He probably saw it as a chance to earn a permanent commission in the Royal Air Force, an attractive alternative to returning to Glace Bay and a job in the pit. Raymond Collishaw probably influenced the outcome since he, while Edwards was in a German prison camp, had been involved in planning the creation of the Canadian Air Force. Despite this planning Collishaw remained in the RAF where he rose to the rank of air vice-marshal. Edwards, however, was demobilized from the RAF and immediately returned to Canada where he joined the Canadian Air Force.

Initially Edwards was at a disadvantage. His formal education had ended at the age of fourteen in New Aberdeen and, after 1924, virtually all officers commissioned into the Royal Canadian Air Force as it had become, were graduates of the Royal Military College of Canada. Experience helped him to success and his wartime service in the RNAS and the RAF were appreciated. In 1937 he commanded the RCAF detachment at the coronation of King George VI in London and at the beginning of the Second World War was senior staff officer engaged in highly confidential business between Ottawa and New York helping neutral Americans join the allies as flyers. This was illegal and both the American and Canadian governments kept the enterprise at arms length. The contact between the civilian entrepreneurs and government was Gus Edwards by then a Group Captain and operating under the cover name of Mr. P Jones.

The rapid expansion of the RCAF meant rapid promotion for the competent and by 1941 Edwards was an Air Vice Marshal and, based in London, the air officer in charge of all RCAF overseas. He suffered during this period from ill health and was passionately committed to the full Canadianization of all RCAF squadrons rather than the intermingling of British and Canadian flyers and ground crew. It was a contentious issue involving government policy and tempers were soon frayed. In a memorandum of the period Edwards was described as "the most forceful man in the RCAF". In soon resulted in what became known as "the Battle of Bloody Nonsense" and it did Edwards no good.

In an "off the record" briefing to visiting journalists Edwards criticized the editorial policy of several Canadian newspapers, the *Montreal Gazette* and the *Globe and Mail*. "Some people" he said, "are talking a lot of bloody nonsense about splitting the Empire. If Canadians who see it from that point of view want to be mugs all their lives, that's their business." The remark was leaked. The offended press had a field day and the government was rattled. Chided the *Ottawa Journal* pompously, "Apart altogether from his bad language, it looks to us as though Air Officer in Chief Edwards should keep his mouth shut about government policy."

Years later it appears that the weight of logic was on the side of Edwards. He should not have commented on government policy but he trusted the press reporters not to leak comments made "off the record". His involvement made the debate still more acrimonious. The Canadian and British governments made their peace over the issue but, according High Commissioner Vincent Massey, the Canadian Chief of Air Staff "very nearly had to disown" Edwards.

Edwards retired early, at the age of fifty-nine, probably due to ill health, and in 1944 returned to Canada. He did not return to live in Glace Bay but chose a small community in Quebec. After some years of illness he moved to Scotsville in Arizona where, a few months later, in February, 1952, he died.

COLONIAL LOGS SET SAIL

Sydney Harbour played a critical role in both the First and Second World War. Harbour defenses were constructed to ensure that neither submarines nor enemy surface vessels could penetrate and cause havoc in the convoys assembled there to carry supplies to England. Throughout the Second World War convoys formed up here, designated SC convoys either denoting that they were from Sydney or that they were slow convoys. Halifax convoys were designated HFX.

The convoy system in the First World War did not begin until 1917. The centralized control of convoy operations was in the hands of Rear Admiral Bertram M.Chambers. He arrived in Sydney on 3 October, 1917 and set up his headquarters at the now semi-abandoned offices of the *Sydney Post* on Dorchester Street.

Chambers was lauded at war's end for his success that he attributed to the magnificent harbour at Sydney and the unstinting co-operation from Canadians. Once ships left Sydney Harbour they faced the hazards of weather and enemy action that had to be overcome if supplies of food and war material were reach its destination. There was concern about submarines. Initially there had been little worry that they would harm shipping on the East Coast. They probably would not be able to sail that far. But in October, 1916 a German U-boat sailed into Newport, Rhode Island, showed off its armaments and boasting its lack of need to refuel, sailed off again where it sank five allied ships off Nantucket Island. Because of American neutrality the U.S. Navy could do little except rescue survivors. By 1917 the menace of U-boats was extreme, more then two thousand four hundred allied and neutral ships were lost to them. The convoy system reduced losses enormously but even in 1918 more than one thousand ships were lost. But, regardless of all the fears, the demand for war materials remained insatiable. What follows is the sad story of a brave effort that failed; of a "ship" that set off for Britain alone.

One item of war material that is not generally recognized but was essential to the war effort was logs. While oil was used to power some warships there was still a heavy dependence upon coal to fire the boilers of both warships and merchant vessels. The coal mines of Britain were all underground and while there was plenty of coal the cost of production steadily rose. The cost of timber and stores, for example was by 1919 double what it had been in 1917. Timber is needed to shore up the roof of mine tunnels so that they do not collapse as they advance to and along the coalface.

In the early years of the war this timber, the pit props, came from Scandinavia but this supply was being slowed by German submarine action and the volume required was increasing. The British government sought new sources and advertised in newspapers in Canada and Newfoundland, then a colony. North Sydney entrepreneur, Ivan Bayley, who contacted London and eventually received an order from a combination of British collieries, saw one such advertisement. The order was initially for seven thousand cords. It is a reasonable assumption that one cord will produce around forty sturdy props. With a prop every two feet on each side of the roadway forty props, the yield of a cord will cover about eighty feet of roadway – not including overhead supports – so seven thousand will allow the construction of more than a hundred miles.

There were two problems he had to overcome. First, he had to cut the logs. Secondly, he had to get the logs across the Atlantic – Cardiff in South Wales was the likely destination.

Answers to both problems lay in Newfoundland. There were ample and suitable logs near Bonne Bay in western Newfoundland and a small logging community of Lomond, now in the Gros Morne National Park, and the harbour at Bonne Bay was sufficiently sheltered for a massive raft of logs to be constructed there.

Bayley drew up plans, patented his blueprint under the name of "Bayley Marine Freight Transport", lined up a 250 hp marine engine from the United States and sought financial backing. Before he could get this backing word came from England of a change of plans. There was now no longer need, as there had been in the initial plan, for cargo space and an engine. What was more, they need extra logs so the requirement was upped to eight thousand cords. When the raft was near completion the British would send across an ocean-going tug to pull it over. By early in 1917 Bayley had formed a company, "The Globe Timber and Transportation Co". He and several men from North Sydney headed for Bonne Bay, Newfoundland.

Construction could probably be described as basic engineering. The logs were simply tied together with cable and iron chains and secured with various sizes of iron rods, all welded together. Forty men worked building the raft. The felling of trees began 17 March, 1917. The weight of the iron rods alone was twenty tons.

Almost a year later the raft was ready and a Dutch ocean-going tug, *The Leburdee,* was on hand. Holland was neutral in the First World War but the Germans had established a practice of attacking and sinking any ship they wished. The raft began its long journey but not long after reaching open sea and just off Cape Anguille on the south-west corner of Newfoundland it was hit by a massive storm and some of the logs began to break off. There was no other choice but to seek shelter for repairs in Sydney Harbour where they anchored off the Marine Railway Yard for repairs. It took a week but then all was ready for the trans-Atlantic crossing.

Ivan Bayley and his wife stood proudly on the deck for pictures – they did not accompany it on the voyage – and the tug pulled it away from the shelter of the harbour in the middle of March. A couple of days later Bayley received a message from the tug. "All's Well".

The *Sydney Daily Post* reported on March 21 that nothing had been heard from another steamer, the *Sagona* out of St. John's nor had they any information about the plight of many in the sealing fleet. There was no mention of the raft but it and its tug along with the other vessels had been struck by a massive storm. Ivan Bayley's raft was never heard of again.

BERYL MARKHAM – "STRAIGHT ON TILL MORNING"

It is strange, albeit gratifying for many Cape Bretoners, that Beryl Markham, who led a life as dramatic and varied as can be imagined, should be best remembered as the aviatrix (that's what female fliers were once called) who reached her pinnacle of fame in a bog close to the shore near Baleine. She, a female Peter Pan, found her "Never-never land" here. She was only on Cape Breton for a day and night yet it was the high point of her career and briefly made Cape Breton the focus of world attention.

A biography was written of Beryl Markham by Mary Lovell entitled <u>Straight on Till Morning</u> undoubtedly derived from the words of Peter Pan whose directions to never-never land were "take the second star to the right and straight on till morning". Is it too far fetched to see the life of Beryl Markham as that of a would-be Peter Pan, someone who wouldn't grow up? Beryl, born into an upper class English family was a wild child raised on a farm in Africa after her mother left her with her father. She was a pioneer flier taking safari hunters out into the bush. She married three times, was divorced for infidelity and her lovers included Isak Denison's husband, Bror Blixen, Denys Finch Hatton (admirably played by Robert Redford in the movie Out of Africa) and Prince Henry, Duke of Gloucester and King George VI's brother. She was a legendary beauty whose eighty-four years were lived fully. But it was her association with Cape Breton that catapulted her from being simply an upper class philanderer with a taste for airplanes into the history books of aviation. She went straight on till morning and found her never-never land on Cape Breton.

The train of events that led to her world fame began at a dinner party in London in March of 1936. She had flown Baron von Blixen from Nairobi and was dining with an English aristocrat with an unsavory reputation named John Carberry. Carberry's second wife had been killed when her plane cashed – though some said it was suicide to escape Carberry's cruelty – and his third wife (he married her when she was seventeen and he close to forty) brought up the subject of trans-Atlantic flight. This may well have been because Beryl's current lover was well-known pilot Jimmy Mollison who had earlier flown east to west across the Atlantic from Ireland. His was the only single-handed non-stop flight across the Atlantic in that direction. No woman had crossed the Atlantic that way although Amelia Earhart had flown the so-called easy way across, west to east, landing in Ireland after a relatively short fifteen hours.

It was at this party that the idea was circulated. Beryl Markham should try to be the first woman, east to west across the Atlantic. Carberry agreed to finance the flight. The plane, to be named *The Messenger*, would be a Vega Gull powered by a 200 hp De Haviland Gipsy Six engine. It would be fitted with the new French variable pitch propellers and would be built at the Gravesend plant of Percival

Aircraft. For three months Beryl flew almost daily from London down the Thames to Gravesend to watch construction. Extra fuel tanks were fitted to increase the range of the Gull from 660 miles to 3,600 miles.

On the afternoon of 4 September, despite melancholy weather forecasts and attempts to have her postpone her undertaking, Markham, according to reports, "clearly frightened", took off in bad weather, "a flying petrol can". Her only supplies were sandwiches and bars of chocolate. Said Jimmy Mollison to Percival, "Well, that's the last we shall see of her".

In fact, the last sight of her from England was by a *Daily Mirror* photographer who had taken up another plane and somewhere over Somerset gave her a final wave, which she returned. She was next sighted off Castletown, County Cork, Ireland. From then on, nothing but hours of silence and tension among the thousands who, by way of newspaper reports, had taken up the vigil.

Later, Markham described some of her ordeal. "I really had a terrible time. That's the only word for it – terrible. I knew I was for it half an hour after I left. I pulled out my chart of the Atlantic, and a gust of wind blew it out of my hand". She flew on through driving rain, strong winds and an electrical storm. Several hours later the crew of the steamship *Spaardam* sighted her plane a hundred miles off the coast of Newfoundland. Next, it was sighted flying over Renews at the southeast tip of Newfoundland. When this news was received a large welcoming crowd began to assemble at Floyd Bennett Field, Long Island, New York. They were to be temporarily disappointed.

Markham, believing that she was running out of fuel, first hoped to land at Harbour Grace but heavy fog there made that impossible.

She decided to head for Sydney Airport but as her plane lost height and she became more convinced that her fuel tank was close to empty, she sighted land. Cape Breton.

Willie Vincent Burke saw the Gull circling over Baleine, a dozen miles short of Sydney Airport, looking for a landing spot at around 11.30 on Saturday morning, 5 September. Others may have seen it at much the same time. Children of the Perry family also spotted it. Mrs. "Bud" Bagnell (nee Regina Gallant) was eleven years old at the time and living in Little Lorraine. She remembers seeing the plane circling and her father saying "That plane's in trouble". She and her father took the family truck to where they thought it had landed and remembers seeing people helping Mrs. Markham out of the cockpit – "the way the nose was stuck in the mud it was almost impossible for her to have got out by herself. I recollect a ladder and men carrying her from the plane on it. She was bleeding from a cut on her forehead." The people from Baleine carried her to the Perry home where she washed and had a hot drink. She then crossed to the Burke's home nearby and phoned Louisbourg.

Edith MacInnis, operating the exchange that was located in her own home, received the call. "This is Beryl Markham; I've landed at Baleine. Could you send a taxi down for me?" Edith MacInnis remembered that there were no taxis in Louisbourg at that time, "So I phoned George Lewis – he had one of the only ten cars in town - and he set off straight away. Then I phoned Dr. (Freeman) O'Neill (Dr O'Neill was keenly interested in airplanes and had speculated that Mrs. Markham might land in Sydney to refuel) I told him what had happened. That was the first news anyone had of Mrs. Markham landing. My cousin then was working in Schenectady, New York, and suddenly he heard it coming over the radio and that the news had been sent out from Louisbourg by Edith MacInnis. He said he nearly jumped a foot in the air when he heard my name."

George Lewis' son Harvey remembered the events clearly. His father had been buying swordfish down at the wharf when the news reached him from Edith MacInnis. He immediately set off for Baleine and brought Mrs. Markham to their house. News of her arrival had spread fast and crowds were flocking into Louisbourg. Local radio personalities "Mr. Nathanson and Robbie Robertson set up a transmitter in the corner of our living room. Then they got word from New York that the Hearst people in New York had exclusive rights to the story and would sue if Nathanson broadcast anything. Nathanson replied that that they were all set up and there would be a nationwide broadcast whatever Hearst said. If Markham couldn't speak then he – Nathanson – would go on the air and tell North America that Markham had arrived, was in the house with him, but that Hearst would sue if she spoke. The Hearst crowd decided that would be really bad publicity and relented."

Within no time Louisbourg was swarming with people coming in from across the country. The Crowdis Hotel was not big and was soon filled. Edith MacInnis remembered that people camped out all over town and slept out on peoples' balconies and that the people in town prepared food for them. "The telephone exchange normally closed down at 9 pm but the volume of the business from all over North America so we kept operating all night. None of us in the house went to bed that night. Those who weren't operating the phone were making sandwiches for all the people who poured into town. The normal daily load in Louisbourg was thirty five calls. From 3.30 pm to 10.30 pm that Saturday we handled 164 toll calls – and there were still more coming through the night".

Robbie Robertson from CJCB Radio got to the Lewis house to prepare for the broadcast. It would be carried by three networks – the Canadian Radio Corporation, the British Broadcasting Corporation and an American station. Frank Willis, who had achieved some fame earlier covering the Moose River Mine disaster, flew in from Halifax to do the interview.

Eva Lewis was home when Mrs. Markham reached the house. "I gave her tea and toast. The first thing she did was phone New York and lots of other people. The house was soon full of people so we were busy making tea and coffee. Frank Willis and Mr. Nathanson made their broadcast and then Mrs. Markham went to bed. Mrs. Markham was really charming. She mixed in with everyone and got on well with them all. She borrowed a pair of George's pajamas. She got up at 5 am on Sunday morning and George and I drove her to the airport." Representatives of Kings Feature Services, who had her story rights, insisted that she have a paper bag over her head so that no unauthorized person could photograph her.

Beryl Markham flew by small plane to Halifax then on to New York. Five thousand cheered her into Floyd Bennett Field and thousands more waved and shouted their support as a screaming motorcycle escort carried her to the Ritz Carlton Hotel in the city.

While Beryl Markham enjoyed the adulation of New York – which had christened her "the blonde sparrow" work began in Louisbourg to rescue her plane.

Crowds of people came out from Sydney to see the plane before it was loaded onto a scow and transported to Louisbourg. Ray Goodwin, pilot-instructor of the Cape Breton Flying Club, was in charge and had more than fifteen men working at it for eleven days. He had first thought to have the plane hauled to the road but that was too far off. The seashore was closer, about a hundred yards, and it was dragged there over a road of boards. From Louisbourg it was to be trucked to Halifax. This plan fell through. The plane made the truckload wider than permitted and the Department of Highways refused to issue a special permit. So instead it was loaded onto another vessel and towed to Pier 23 in Halifax. From there it traveled onto England and later East Africa where John Carberry, who owned it, sold it to an East Indian entrepreneur. It was left abandoned at an airfield near Dar es Salaam and slowly rotted away.

Meanwhile Beryl Markham had a triumphant return to England aboard the *Queen Mary*. Later she returned to the States, married again, divorced again and returned to Kenya to become a successful horse race trainer. Coincidentally, one of her horses competed against a horse owned Bill Holmes, who was working in Africa and who some years later became manager of CJCB TV.

In 1985, in her eighties and rumoured to be living off orange juice and vodka, she lived in a borrowed bungalow near Nairobi. A member of the Canadian High Commission staff in Nairobi, Margo Schwartz, knowing that her father Irving had seen the *Messenger* at Baleine nearly half a century earlier, arranged for him to visit. Later they lunched at the racecourse and reminisced about the events on Cape Breton.

In 1986 RAF Abington, the field from which she had taken off, wanted to celebrate the fiftieth anniversary of her departure. There would be numerous sponsors for the celebration, including the Province of Nova Scotia. It was not to be. Pottering in her garden she fell and broke her hip. She died of pneumonia on 3 August.

A packed crowd attended her memorial service in London where it was said of her in tribute, "Like a comet she lit up all around her".

THREE WRITERS

Few today read the works of the one time distinguished American author, Charles Dudley Warner, but he was the first great booster for Cape Breton. He is now best known, if at all, for <u>The Gilded Age</u>, written in 1874, in collaboration with Mark Twain. Well before he took to writing he had been a surveyor for the rail lines pushing westward across Missouri and it was perhaps this that gave him a taste for travel. He later wrote of traveling on the Nile, of wandering in Eastern Europe, of riding horseback through the southern United States, of the Levant, of Italy and parts of Canada. But one piece, originally published in serial form in "*Atlantic Monthly*", would have a most profound effect on Cape Breton and even on its economic development. Entitled <u>Baddeck and That Sort of Thing</u>, it prompted Helen Keller to comment in her book, <u>The Story of My Life</u> "…I have spent many happy days with (Alexander Graham Bell) at Washington and at his beautiful home in the heart of Cape Breton Island, near Baddeck, the village made famous by Charles Dudley Warner's book…"

Warner's book put Baddeck, and ultimately the rest of Cape Breton, on the map of desirable destinations. Some of his writings will, to modern readers, appear lugubrious. But his description of the approach to the village, seeing the Watchabaktehkt Hills(sic) across the water, and then on along the shore resembled our own memories of the same route taken almost a hundred years later. "Before dark we had crossed the Middle River and the Big Baddeck on long wooden bridges which straggled over sluggish waters and long reaches of marsh…As dusk came on, we crossed the last hill, and were bowling along beside the still gleaming water. Lights began to appear in infrequent farm houses, and under cover of the gathering night seemed to be stately mansions, and we fancied we were on a noble highway…about to be driven into a town of wealth and a port of great commerce. We were, nevertheless, anxious about Baddeck. What sort of haven would we reach after our heroic week of travel? Would the hotel be like that at Plaster Cove?"

Any trepidation Warner had was soon dispelled. "The hotel was a large one and we enjoyed the luxury of spacious rooms, an abundant supper and a friendly welcome; in short, we found ourselves at home. The proprietor of the Telegraph House is the superintendent of the land lines of Cape Breton, a Scotchman, of course; but his wife is a Newfoundland lady. We cannot violate the sanctity of what seemed like private hospitality by speaking freely of this lady and her lovely daughters, whose education has been so admirably advanced in the excellent school in Baddeck; but we can confidently advise any American who is going to Newfoundland, to get a wife there, if he wants one at all. It is the only article he can bring from the Province that he will not have to pay duty on."

It was while heading to Newfoundland – though not in search of a wife – that Alexander Graham Bell diverted his journey to visit Baddeck and satisfy the curiosity that Warner's book had raised in him.

Alexander Graham Bell may or may not have been the first American to summer on the island. But the Bell family certainly gave a tremendous fillip to the fashion of seasonal travel northwards. Since the Bells put Baddeck firmly on the map of agreeable destinations many scores have come to Cape Breton to relish the wonderful scenery and to provide employment, social variety and friendship to many thousands of permanent residents. They have ranged from German industrialists to President Eisenhower's pastor. We initially came came here as a summer resident, though hardly from the prosperous ranks of those who are generally in that category.

But there were two who made an indelible impact upon us. One was an Englishman, resident of Washington, the other the grandson of one of Cape Breton's pioneer families who had become a distinguished journalist in New York.

We had only been on our farm a few months when a tall aristocratic looking Englishman came to our door. In those days I thought him rather elderly – he was just sixty but I was twenty-five – and he was most amiable. He introduced himself as Eddie Russell and told us he had a home at Pony's Point, between Iona and Washabuckt. He gave us our first goat and also told us that he knew something of plumbing but since, at that time we had no running water, we were unable to make use of his skills. Despite our age difference we quickly became friends, even allowing us to take a bath when we visited.

Edward Wriothesley Curzon Russell came up every summer from Washington and he clearly regarded himself not so much as a summer visitor but as a resident of the area; over the years I gained the impression that he was more in the company of permanent residents than American summer residents. He had visitors from the States. I remember one landed his small plane in one of the Russell's fields. Eddie Russell wasn't an American – except perhaps by naturalization – but an Englishman. A genuinely aristocratic one at that. His father, Lord Ampthill had been Governor of Bengal and, for seven months whilst Lord Curzon was away, Viceroy of India. Eddie was born in India in June of 1901, something he said which had hindered his being granted a visa into the United States – he said that although he could prove he was conceived in England it didn't cut any ice with the Americans. Eddie's aristocratic credentials were impressive – although he never told us of them and we discovered them many years later. His mother, formerly Lady Lygon, was the daughter of the Earl of Beauchamp and Lady-in-Waiting to the Queen Mother Mary, widow of King George V.

Eddie was also an age that probably saved his life. He was just too young to have fought in the First World War – when to a greater extent than others the aristocratic class was butchered in the early months on the Western Front – and he was too old for a combat role in the Second World War. Instead he became British Air Attache in Washington with the rank of Air Commodore and the eventual receipt of the Order of the British Empire (OBE).

It was during the war that he took a train from Washington to Ottawa, or so he told me, and met on the journey, also on some military business, a young woman named Barbara Korff whom he married in Washington in 1941, just two months before America entered the war. Barbara's father was the Russian Baron Serge Korff – Barbara was born in Helsingfors where her father was a professor at the university – and after the Russian Revolution Korff was appointed Lieutenant Governor of Finland. The Bolshevik *coup d'etat* ended that, and he and his family fled to the United States where he became an acknowledged authority on international affairs and a professor at Columbia University and at the Georgetown School of Foreign Service until his death.

The Russell family – there are two daughters, Diana and Margaret Angela – were familiar faces on Cape Breton long before we came here and had many friends in the Iona area. One of the girls – although she has probably mercifully blanked out her memory of it - briefly helped us cut pulp on Cains Mountain. Later, in the 1970s, after the Highland Heights Inn was opened, Barbara sold a number of her watercolours on display there with the proceeds given to the Inn.

After a couple of years living on Cain's Mountain we had running water. Eddie told us with some pride that he was a fully qualified plumber and a paid up member of the union. He would install the hot water heater, which apparently he would also supply. With great competence we soon had running water, hot and cold. He refused to charge us anything – even for the water heater – but insisted we not tell the union.

We exchanged books and we were really impressed when we found that he was working on one of his own. Design For Destiny, published by Ballantine Books in New York in 1971 was praised by Colin Wilson who regarded it as "one of the most important books of the year". It expressed Eddie's deeply religious, though rather unconventional, philosophy of life. At the end of the book are the lines "these final pages are written at the end of a rough, little known road. Though the road ends here the forest stretches on climbing ridge on ridge. With its promise of further trails to explore, of further adventures of the mind and body, of endless, unguessed horizons stretching upward to the sky, surely the forest is symbolic of the adventure of life?" Eddie told us he wrote the words just after walking part of the Washabuckt road to his home at Pony's Point. He would later write two other books, <u>Report on Radionics</u> and <u>Prospects for Eternity; Debunking Death.</u> Prior to the war Eddie had been managing editor of the *"London Morning Post"*.

During the formative years of the Nova Scotia Highland Village at Iona, Eddie gave practical help. In 1958 he contacted administrators at Colonial Williamsburg in Virginia and Old Sturbridge Village in Massachusetts. They sent him by-law and incorporation information and, using them, Eddie drew up provisional regulations that later, after discussion and modification, were used for the formal incorporation of the Highland Village. The Russells also donated three hundred acres of their property, known as the Barra Forest to the community of Iona. It lies between the Provincial MacCormick Day Park to the north of Iona and their own land near MacAskills Harbour .

Eddie was working on the roof of his home in the United States in his eighty first year. I understand he slipped and fell and died of an aneurysm an hour later. He was a good friend to many on Cape Breton. Though the island has had numerous summer residents from the States dating back to before the Bells, I warrant there were few more warmly regarded than he. He was missed by far more than his immediate family.

In the years during which we lived in New York City we devoured any writings we could find about Nova Scotia generally and Cape Breton in particular. The book that utterly enthralled us was <u>The Highland Heart of Nova Scotia</u> by Neil MacNeil, another former newspaper managing editor. Neil MacNeil first came to Cape Breton as a child to stay on his grandfather's farm at Washabuckt. Neil's father, a building contractor, had to travel frequently so Neil and his brother were sent to live on grandfather's farm during their impressionable years. The Highland Heart of Nova Scotia was the product of those years and it told tales, often tall, of the Gaelic speaking Barra Scots "who feared neither man nor the devil". It was not published until 1948 when Neil MacNeil was fifty-seven and a glow of affection and nostalgia warms the pages. The book has in it the breath of life. In its pages the *S.S. Marion* sails to Little Narrows again and a tall-talking gourmet struggles to roast a loon. Tales are told over bannock and tea and biblical stories have wonderful interpretation.

Aside from this book, Neil MacNeil led a distinguished life. After graduation from St. Francis Xavier University in 1912 he joined the *Montreal Daily Mail* as a ten dollar a week cub reporter. The following year he joined the staff of the *Montreal Gazette*. On assignment a few years later in New York he came to the attention of the *New York Times* which hired him as a copy editor. He stayed with the *Times* until his retirement where he rose to the post of assistant night managing editor. During this period he became fascinated by reports of the excavations in Egypt, particularly those of King Tut-ankh-Amen. Neil MacNeil and the then managing editor who directed the handling of the stories competed to see which could assimilate the most archeological lore. "Mr. MacNeil, who as a boy had braved the frustrations of learning Gaelic, eventually was able to transliterate and often translate ancient Egyptian hieroglyphics." These efforts not only won praise from experts but also earned him the nickname "King Tut".

After retirement in 1951 Neil MacNeil agreed to serve as editorial director of the Hoover Commission and upon the death of the former President Herbert Hoover he became one of Mr. Hoover's three literary executors. Neil MacNeil wrote a number of other books and was a frequent public speaker. He was a President of the International Friends of the Antigonish Movement and was for several years president of the Clan MacNeil Association of America.

He died in 1969 at the age of seventy-eight. He wrote several books but for the general readers and those of us on Cape Breton his <u>Highland Heart</u> is the one most warmly remembered.

TOM KENT - OK, SIGNED TK

In the mid 1970s, driving through the countryside of Cape Breton with Tom Kent, then President of the Cape Breton Development Corporation (DEVCO), I was briefly lost. "When in doubt" said my passenger, "turn left" Was he expressing a political philosophy? No, it was instead his approach to auto orienteering. Many thought he was of the political left but it would be nearer the truth to describe him of the extreme centre, a most liberal Liberal who once ran, unsuccessfully as a Liberal, against the NDP leader Tommy Douglas.

TK, as he was known to friends and co-workers, may have used the "turn left" approach to driving but he never, so far as I was aware, was lost as he and his wife Phyllida toured the roads of the island, determined to know every inch of it. In his red MG sports car and with a pipe firmly clenched between his teeth, the two of them were intent on knowing all that could be discovered. Though both to the eye and the ear quintessentially English they were and are thoroughly Canadian. Less than a decade earlier, in 1966, events on the island triggered legislation that brought them here from Ottawa and made Cape Breton their home. Initially home was an apartment in Cabot

House in Sydney, later a house in a delightful valley near Mabou in the western highlands.

!966 was a bleak year for Cape Breton. A report on the coal industry, called the Donald Report made a forecast for the coal industry that cast a pall of gloom over the island. It articulated what many had for years feared. After centuries of mining coal the Donald Report put an end-date on the industry.

Yet former Englishman Tom Kent turned the report from a death knell into a challenge. The light at the end of the tunnel was not simply the train bearing down on a helpless community. It was a beacon of opportunity.

Tom Kent was not only a former Englishman, he was a former many things; among them, a former member of wartime British Intelligence; according to his entry in the Canadian Who's Who this work was for both the War Office and Foreign Office and, though he told me nothing of this, the intelligence body that reported directly to the Foreign Office was the SIS or Secret Intelligence Service, more generally known as MI6. He was well qualified having won a 1st Class Honours degree in modern "Greats" at Corpus Christi College, Oxford. During these war years he met Phyllida Cross who was working at the top secret Bletchley Hall where the German Enigma code was cracked. They married in June, 1944.

Following the war he became an editorial writer on the *Manchester Guardian* and after that, Assistant Editor of the *London Economist*. The offer of the editorship of the *Winnipeg Free Press* brought the Kents to Canada. Later a number of roles in Ottawa for the government ranged from TK being Special Consultant to the Right Honorable Lester Pearson, Programming and Policy Secretary to the Prime Minister and

Deputy Minister of Manpower and Immigration and the Department of Regional Economic Expansion. It was in this role that I, and most Cape Bretoners first met him, but shortly after he was appointed President of the Cape Breton Development Corporation. Then we islanders got to know him better.

An Ottawa mandarin with a donnish air, a dry, deliberate and remorseless manner of speaking, his slightly superior manner concealed a dry humour. Of greater importance to Cape Breton, he was an intellectual civil servant with a clear vision of what role the government should take in mitigating the anguish caused by economic evolution.

The Donald Report, or more formally the Report on the Cape Breton Coal Problem, clarified the issues and suggested solutions. The problem was simple. The Dominion Coal and Steel Corporation (DOSCO) could only sustain its operations and provide employment for seven thousand people because of federal financial subsidies. In the year prior to the report these subsidies amounted to $22 million. The subsidies had begun in the 1920s and continually risen save for a brief decline in later years of the Second World War and the immediate aftermath. They escalated dramatically after 1947. By 1965 the annual subvention had risen to close to $3,000 for every coal-mine employee in Nova Scotia.

The reasons were primarily twofold. The mines of Cape Breton follow coal seams that extend out under the ocean. The more coal mined the further the coalface is from the surface and higher the cost of getting it out. At the same time the market for coal was declining. Trains, once coal powered, were now fueled by diesel. The major market for industrial coal was in Quebec and Ontario and federal financial assistance was necessary if the cost of the coal there was to meet the competition for imported oil. Oil was now the preferred fuel for keeping homes warm.

Locally the industry had become accustomed to decades of financial assistance. Money from Ottawa had kept the industry alive since the twenties. Why, local politicians, miners and the general public asked, could it not simply continue? After all it was argued, the various costs, particularly social, could be even greater in the inconceivable event that the entire community be simply abandoned. Yet those costs were escalating at an alarming rate and market forces cannot be ignored. The challenge had become one of not indefinitely supporting with ever larger grants and subsidies but of reducing the harsh impacts of decline on the industry and creating alternative employment opportunities. In short, to lessen the social disruption caused by economic change.

The Cape Breton Development Corporation (DEVCO) was formed to grapple with this task by taking over the mines from the private operator, reducing employment levels gradually, that is, phasing operations down, and creating alternative employment opportunities. Tom Kent was at this time Deputy Minister of Regional Economic Expansion and intimately involved in the creation of DEVCO. In a sense it was his baby and when, after three years it was clear that the baby had real growth problems - particularly a lack of clarity in its pursuit of new economic development - Kent was appointed in 1971 its second president and Chief Operating Officer. In the meantime further setbacks had occurred. On 13 October, 1967, "Black Friday", DOSCO abandoned the steel plant forcing the provincial government into ownership to avoid economic disaster.

Despite setback and a growing public concern that the effort to induce new industrial growth was often simply throwing money away – the infamous Glace Bay heavy water plant was not the only disappointment – there was a major international development that assisted our coal industry. Early in the 1970s OPEC triggered a rapid inflation in oil prices. This made coal more attractive for generating electricity even though the federal government subsidized the cost of imported oil into eastern Canada. But the need remained for greater efficiency in the mines and this resulted in the opening of a new colliery, Lingan, while at the same time closing one that had run out, and building a coal wash plant that made Cape Breton coal more desirable in both the electrical power and international markets.

Tom Kent did great work for the coal miners. He not only extended the life of the industry, he also instituted a non-contributory pension plan for miners as well as a voluntary contributory plan with previous DOSCO employment taken into account. Yet for those not directly involved with mining it was his approach to new developments that created optimism and a very real sense among many hundreds of islanders that they could participate in economic renewal and that decline was not inevitable. It is a sense that, though battered, continues today.

Less visibly Phyllida Kent made her own impact on the island, particularly among the younger generation. Whilst TK was in Ottawa it would have been simple for her to embrace the social life available to the wife of a senior civil servant. Instead, Phyllida Kent entered Carleton University and pursued further studies. Consequently she was able to teach at the University College of Cape Breton (now Cape Breton University).

Early efforts at economic diversification were not successful. Most new enterprises had little relationship to the island's attributes – the pulp and paper plant at Port Hawkesbury was a welcome exception. Small-scale entrepreneurship would have to be carefully nurtured here because there was little experience of it. For a century the region was dominated by coal and steel and what little entrepreneurship there was focused on retailing, construction, farming and the fishery. TK was determined to make changes. The people hired by the corporation to institute changes were not distant middle-level bureaucrats trained in the arts of verbal obfuscation, they were locals sensitive to the aspirations of the community and good communicators in their own right – a prominent radio and television personality, a well-known teacher, and a newspaper columnist among them.

Simply put, the function of the development division of the corporation was to generate local industry that would either manufacture items for export or replace imports. In the primary economic sector farmers were encouraged to improve the quality of their stock. Marine farming – encouraged by the early enterprise of the Mi'kmaq Indians of Eskasoni in oyster raising – was expanded and experiments in raising trout and salmon in nets suspended in salt water were begun. In the manufacturing sector small-scale projects were encouraged and great impetus was given to the craft industry. There was considerable promotion of the tourism potential. Cape Breton has two major visual assets: its magnificent scenery and the Fortress of Louisbourg reconstruction. Greater numbers of tourists, particularly but not exclusively from south of the border, would generate local wealth or, as one wag put it, " Help keep Cape Breton green; bring dollars" To this end a Bed and Breakfast program was begun, walking trails developed, promotion expanded. The examination of new ideas was vigorously encouraged and when put on paper by their innovators for consideration those which merited it received a response that became famous among employees. "OK" signed TK.

For a few brief shining years optimism was widespread. Tourist numbers increased, Cape Breton oysters and trout made their market appearance, sheep were imported from Scotland, a farm flourished near Mabou, allotment gardens sprang up adjacent to industrial towns, a large hydroponics greenhouse pumped out tomatoes and cucumbers, craft production expanded, small processing and manufacturing enterprises were started or expanded.

These efforts alone could not make a major impact on the high unemployment numbers. If major new industry was to succeed an educated and trained workforce was necessary. DEVCO encouraged and assisted in the establishment of the University College of Cape Breton that included in its calendar not only the courses leading to the traditional degrees but also technological programs.

Tom Kent's years as president ended in 1977 though he continued as a board member until 1982. He then sought to rectify an even more intractable problem, that of the steel plant, by this time a provincial crown corporation. The Cape Breton Development Corporation ceased to have a development function. After the election of a new government in 1984 it became a coal company without any broad responsibility for the island economy

Today mines and steel plant have gone. But Tom Kent's efforts to slow social disruption caused by rapid economic change were successful. The levels of individual entrepreneurship are higher, there is far greater diversity of enterprise, optimism is allied to pragmatism and in their bones Cape Bretoners feel that whatever challenges the future holds, they can be overcome. What a far cry from 1967. The coal mines have closed, the steel plant has disappeared. But these events occurred thirty years after they were first envisioned. This breathing spell that enabled us to prepare for our uncertain future was in large part due to the vision and planning of TK.

OK.

EPILOGUE

It was the opening of the steel plant at the start of the twentieth century that broke down the floodgates. Immigrants arrived from Eastern Europe and the Middle East as well as from Britain and the States..

Before we came to settle our four hundred acres in the middle of the island well-established and experienced Dutch farmers had been making a strong positive influence on the island's dairy industry with others later into vegetable and egg production.

Brits and Yanks no longer dominated, though many still arrived. War brides, doctors, steel-makers, mining specialists came from the United Kingdom. From the United States there were entrepreneurs and university professors, journalists, artists, Vietnam War protestors; even so-called hippies came though few of those lasted longer than the first winter.

They may not, as did we, have started without electricity or running water. They did not need to know how much snow to melt to make a cup of tea yet they may have faced their own challenges and may have occasionally yearned for an easier – and warmer – experience. None of them faced the hardships of the early settlers but all of them left their homes and took the path less traveled. People from around the globe continue to come to Cape Breton to live. Many residents who had earlier left for opportunity further west are coming back as retirees. Most, given the immense disparity or race and religion have kept any nostalgia to themselves, have unified amicably and become examples of decency and civility in Cape Breton's harmonious diversity.

NOTES

PRINCE HENRY SINCLAIR
Andrew Sinclair, former Cambridge academic, has published a book <u>The Sword and the Grail</u> and produced a BBC documentary to advance this theory.
Daily Telegraph UK. 21 February, 2004. <u>Splendor on a Transylvanian Scale</u> by Anne Campbell Dixon.
Monument erected by Allister MacDougall, Town Historian, Westford. Mass.
Bradley, Michael. Holy Grail Across the Atlantic. Houslow Press, Willowdale Ontaio. 1988.
In a letter to the Royal Society of Canada, volume VIII, published 1891, p. 127the Reverend George Patterson says that the cannon, "now in the possession of George Burchell" was dug from the mud about half a mile west of the site of the old Grand Battery by Mr. Thomas Cannington.
Bourinot, J G. <u>Historical and Descriptive Account of the Island of Cape Breton</u>. W Foster Brown and Co, Montreal. 1892.
Letter from Robert Smith, Head of Conservation. Royal Armouries. UK. To Parks Canada
Smith, Robert D. Royal Armouries of London. <u>Wrought-iron swivel guns</u>
The Globe and Mail, Toronto, Sept 17, 1991. "*A prince of a find made in Cape Breton*".
Sunday Times, London, UK. 30 August 1992. Article by Gerald Warner and Ian Birrell.

LORD OCHILTREE, THE FIRST CAPE BRETONER
<u>Encyclopedia Britannica</u>, 1911 Edition.Vol 2.
His date of birth unknown but he was the eldest of three sons and his father died in 1695.
<u>Encyclopedia Britannica</u>. 1911 Edition. Vol 25. The grant was later increased to cover much of Canada.
McCreath, Peter L. "*Sir William Alexander*". In *Sojourn*, June, 1975.
Transactions of the Royal Canadian Institute. <u>Nova Scotia: The Royal Charter of 1621</u>. by Colonel Alexander Fraser LL.D
MacLean T. <u>Baleine Settlement</u>. (Staff Report)

Public Archives of Nova Scotia. <u>Place Names and Places of Nova Scotia</u>. Halifax. 1967.
Nearly a hundred years later the French ship *Le Chameau*, headed for nearby Louisbourg and carrying a fortune in French currency ran aground on the rocks off Baleine with the loss of 310 lives. The treasure was largely recovered in 1965.
Magnusson, Magnus. <u>Chambers Biographical Dictionary</u>.London. 1990.

LORD JEFFREY AMHERST
Kennett, Lee. <u>French Armies of the Seven Years' War</u>. Duke University Press. 2001
Long, JC. <u>Lord Jeffrey Amherst</u>. MacMillan Co. 1933.
Pagden, Anthony. <u>Lords of all the World</u>. Yale University Press 1995.
Wyczynski, Michel. <u>The Expedition of the Second Battalion of the Cambris Regiment to Louisbourg, 1758</u>. Nova Scotia Historical Review, Vol 10, No 2, 1990.
Anderson, Fred. Crucible of War.Alfred A Knopf. New York.2000.

ENSIGN PRENTIES
United Empire Loyalists' Association of Canada. Military Units – Loyalist Units. 84th Regiment of Foot
Ensign Prenties's Narrative<u>. A Castaway on Cape Breton</u>. Edited with An Historical Setting and Notes by G.C. Campbell. Toronto. The Ryerson Press.1968. Original published in London – 1782.
Review- British Museum, *The London Review*, Vol. 67, 1782, p. 153.

WYNYARD AND THE 33rd
From the Colonel, Lord Cornwallis' Company, HM Regiment of Foot (Reenactment)
Private correspondence from Radford Polinsky, colonel of the 33rd reenactment regiment in the United States to the authors, with quotations from the 33rd Regiment history.
Crocker, Dr. Robert. <u>The British Army on Our Island</u>.
The 33rd Regiment left Cape Breton after a year of service here, and was replaced by the Royal Highland 42nd Regiment of Foot (later to be called the 1st Battalion The Black Watch, The Royal Highlanders). The 33rd were subsequently stationed in India and, in 1815 fought at Waterloo. They took part in major actions during the Crimea War and, following major reforms in the British Army were amalgamated with the 76th Regiment to form the Duke of Wellington's West Riding Regiment. Their many battalions fought in both world wars and served in the Korean War. More recently they saw duty with United Nation's forces in Bosnia, Kosovo, Iraq and Afghanistan.

DAVID TAITT - SURVEYOR AND INDIAN AGENT
Surveyors would often be used in British intelligence gathering. Until recently their intelligence organization MI4 and its predecessors and its parallel in Asia, the Survey of India, were responsible for topographical intelligence which meant, not simply making maps but fully reporting on all aspects of the flora, fauna and

human infrastructure in the areas of their responsibility.
Wright, Amos J Jr. The McGillivray and McIntosh Traders. NewSouth Books. Montgomery, Ala.
October 12, 1774, a resolution from St. Paul's Parish, quoted in Cashin. The King's Ranger.
Many Indian leaders among the Creeks at this time were of mixed blood. When much later, Alexander McGillivray visited Washington, Abigail Adams, wife of the vice-president remarked, "he dresses in our own fashion, speaks English like a native…is not very dark (and is) much of a gentleman."
Cashin, Edward The King's Ranger. University of Georgia Press, 1989.
Beaton Institute, UCCB. Taitt to (E Nepean?) MG11 Ai pp 99-101. 18 Sept 1785.
Morgan, Robert. Joseph Frederick Wallet DesBarres and the Founding of the Cape Breton Colony. Revue de Universite d'Ottawa. Footnote 50. Yorke to Campbell, 2 March 1786.
Brown, Richard. History of the Island of Cape Breton.. London, 1896.
Cashin. Lachlan McGillivray, Indian Trader. University of Georgia Press, 1992.

DAVID MATHEWS – THE CANTANKEROUS MAYOR OF NEW YORK CITY
Document of Commissions, p 84. New York Public Library
New York Historical Society archives. entry of 24 June, 1776.
Martin, Tom. Hickey conspiracy in Encyclopedia of the American Revolution. Pp 761-2. Martin also states that three men were hanged and that David Mathews was sentenced to death but I have been unable to verify this. Other sources include participants' diaries and newspaper articles of the times.
George Washington General Orders June 27 1776.
Jones, Thomas. The History of New York During the Revolutionary War. Printed for the New York Historical Society 1879.
Letter in the Kentish Gazette, Canterbury, England. August 17 – 21, 1776.
Lichfield Historical Society. History of Lichfield
A guinea was worth one pound one shilling sterling.
Morgan, Robert J. The Loyalists of Cape Breton, in Cape Breton Historical Essays. College of Cape Breton Press. 1980.

THE BALL BROTHERS – PARADOXES IN AN AGE OF PARADOX
The Ball family was mentioned in Debrett's New Baronatage of England, 1808. Their family home was Stonehouse Court, a Tudor manor near Painswick in Gloucestershire. Stonehouse Court, no longer owned by the family, still stands as a hotel (B and B in 2002 was 42 pounds sterling.)
Memorandum to Rear Admiral of the Red Sir Alexander John Ball, Baronet Blofield.
Timeline of Rear Admiral of the Red, Sir Alexander John Ball.
Elva Jackson notes, Beaton Institute, Cape Breton University
Text extract from written copy housed in the PRO, Kew England.. CO217/113 – folio534 –page 1653.

Donovan, Ken. Slavery After the Conquest in Cape Breton, 1758 – 1815. Chapter 6.
Public Records Office - Kew, England CO217/117, folios 425-432 pages 847-861.
Dictionary of National Biography.
Porter, Roy. England in the Eighteenth Century. Folio Society, London. 1998.
Letter from Ball in prison in Sydney to the Right Honorable Lord Pelham, His Majesty's Principal Secretary of State For the Home Department. October 15th 1801. CO217/119
Dictionary of National Biography, UK – 1880.
History of St John's, Point Edward, written on the 120th anniversary of the building of the church., by the Reverend W K Morrison.

WOODHAUSEN - A CONVICT
Beaton Institute, University College of Cape Breton. St. George's Church Records.
Burke, Charles A. Irish Convicts Abandoned on Cape Breton's Shore, 1788. Cape Breton's Magazine. Issue # 72.
Bailyn, Bernard. Voyagers to the West. Alfred A. Knopf. New York. 1987.
peteblu. http://www.blupete.com History of Nova Scotia. Index of dates. 1733-35
The number of emigrants sailing for North America, including Canada and the West Indies, totaled 9364. The number of convicts transported between 1718 and 1775 from the Home Counties of England (London and its environs) were estimated to number 18,600. A further 16,000 were sent by the courts of Ireland and about 800 from Scotland.
Radzinowitz, L. History of Criminal Law. The Movement for Reform. MacMillan, 1948.
Freeman's Journal, Dublin, 2 October, 1788.
Burke, Charles, Report of the Board of Trustees for the year 1950. Public Archives of Nova Scotia, King's Printer, Halifax NS. 1951.
Burke, Charles. Irish Convicts Abandoned. *Quoting Report in Canadian Archives 1895.*
Public Archives of Nova Scotia PANS 1895
There was one final shipment of convicts that arrived in North America. The ship, *the Duke of Leinster* landed convicts at Bay Bulls, Newfoundland in the summer of 1789. It had set out bound for Australia but because of an outbreak of fever on board the captain had made for the nearest land. Possibly he was also somewhat of course.
Beaton Institute Archives, MG 2.5

CAPTAIN THOMAS CRAWLEY
Brown, Richard. History of the Island of Cape Breton, London, 1896.
Jackson, Elva. Cape Breton and the Jackson Kith and Kin. Lancelot Press, Windsor, NS. 1981.
Moose and caribou co-existed on Cape Breton until the much later introduction of the white tailed deer which resulted in the extinction of the caribou here.
The Constitutional Gazette. "If Honor in the breech is lodged, As Hudibras has shown, It may from thence be fairly judged Sir Peter's Honor's gone."

Morgan, Robert. Early Cape Breton. Breton Books.2000.
Cape Breton Historical Essays. College of Cape Breton Press, 1980. D C Harvey.
Scottish Immigration to Cape Breton.
Morgan, Robert J. CB Historical Essays. *"The Loyalists of Cape Breton"*.

JOHN AND NANCY LEITCH – PRESS-GANGED AND SHIP-WRECKED
Jackson, Elva E. – Cape Breton and the Jackson Kith and Kin. Lancelot Press, Weindsor, NS. 1981.
Guardian of the Gulf. Sydney, Cape Breton and the Atlantic Wars
Tennyson, Brian and Sarty, Roger. Guardian of The Gulf. Chapter One – *"The Outpost of Empire"*. University of Toronto Press. Toronto. Buffalo. London. 2000
Bailyn, Bernard. Voyages to the West. A Passage in the peopling of America on the eve of the Revolution. Alfred A. Knopf. NY. 1987
Press gang information from internet

THANKFULL AND MARY – THE COSSITS AND McLEODS
Morgan, Robert. Early Cape Breton. Breton Books 2000.
Robertson, Eleanor. Loyalist Foods. Shelburne County Genealogical Society. 2000.
Sloane, Eric. The Seasons of America Past. Wilfred Funk Inc. New York.1958.
Canadian National Biography.
The Bishop's visit was a happy occasion for the Ball family and the residents of Northwest Arm since the Bishop had a confirmation service in their community. Although sharing the same surname the many McLeods of Scotland do not necessarily denote a family relationship.
Johnson, Paul. The Birth of Modern. Harper Collins, 1991. p. 219. quoting J.C. Buchanan, Travels in the Western Hebrides.
Grigor, Iain Fraser. Mightier than a Lord. Acair Limited, Stornoway, Lewis. 1979.
McPherson, Flora. Watchman Against the World. Breton Books 1993. Previously published London, 1962.
Bunyan, always in poor health, died in 1838 when he was 21.
Dictionary of National Biography.
Patterson, George G. History of Victoria County. College of Cape Breton Press. 1978.
Newton, Pamela. The Cape Breton Book of Days. UCCB Press, 1984.

MURDER AND THE WASHED UP SAILORS
Beaton Institute Archives, Cape Breton University. MGM, 53
MacKinnon, J.G. Old Sydney. Sketcxhes of the town and its people.

RICHARD BROWN - WHEN COAL BECAME KING
The current Earl of Lonsdale's Lakeland Investments owns, according to North West Business Insider Magazine, 72,000 acres of land.
Encyclopedia Britannica, 1911 Edition, Vol 16.
Fleischman, Richard K and Oldroyd, David. The Development of British and Canadian Coal-Mining Enterprise: A Comparative Study in Costing Methods.

1825-1900.Interdisciplinary Perspectives Conference, Manchester, UK. 2000.
Brown, Richard. The Coal Fields and Coal Trade of the Island of Cape Breton. London, 1871.
Brown, Richard. History of the Island of Cape Breton. London, 1896.
Canadian Mining Journal. March 26, 1920.
Jackson, Elva E. North Sydney, Nova Scotia. Windows on the Past. Mika Publishing Company, Ontario. 1982.
The Royal Navy sometimes objected to using Sydney coal because it gave off a black smoke which made their ships not only visible to the enemy but spoilt the paintwork and discolored the sails. Brown argued vigorously that in times of peace there was no enemy and the relative cheapness of Cape Breton coal over Welsh supplies mitigated against their other argument.
Johnson, Paul. The Birth of Modern. Harper Collins.1991.

THE LONELY LOVER – A TRAVELER'S TALE
Beaton Institute, UCCB.

WILLIAM PENN HUSSEY - HUCKSTER
Correspondence from Office of Finance, Town Hall, Danvers, MA to authors with 1890 biographies of William Penn Hussey and J Fred Hussey
MacDonald, Ned. The Broken Ground: A History of Inverness Town. Chap 8. Beaton Institute. FC 2349 I5. M 34.
Correspondence from Richard Trask, Town Archivist, Danvers to David Newton, author.

PHILIP WORGAN
Faughnan, Thomas. Late Colour-Sergeant 6th Royal Regiment. Stirring Incidents in the Life of a British Soldier. Toronto: Hunter, Rose and Co. 1883.
Schneider, Phyllis Worgan. Ferndell. City Printers, Sydney, 1979.
Sub-Lieutenant Worgan is often referred to with other ranks attached to his name. He was often called Captain and this may have been the consequence of his having been the senior officer on a vessel, probably the *Wolverine* and being customarily referred to as a captain of that ship. He was also referred to as Commander, equivalent to the army rank of Lieutenant Colonel. It is probable that he continued to serve in the reserve and achieved that rank through the passage of time. There is no evidence that he saw active service after coming to Cape Breton
Sydney Record, July 13, 1899, November 28, 1903.
Beaton Institute, UCCB. Bourinot Papers. MG12, 16.
A brief history of the parish of St John the Evangelist Anglican Church of Point Edward.
The St. Mark's Church replaced St. Mark's chapel.
Sadly, the homes mentioned here have gone. The ruins of the McLennan can still be seen at Petersfield Park but the Ingraham home at Westmount was destroyed, Moxham Castle burned down and the Worgan home was demolished.

HENRY MELVILLE WHITNEY - "FINDER OF SYDNEY"
MacGillivray, Don. *Henry Melville Whitney Comes to Cape Breton*. Acadiensis.
Sydney Post. October 2, 1900.

ARTHUR J. MOXHAM - BUILDER OF STEEL PLANTS AND CASTLES
Jessome, Leo. *The Price Paid*. April 3, 1989. Beaton Institute.
Montreal Daily Star, Nov 22, 1899.
"Teamwork" the organ of Dominion Steel and Coal Corporation, Ltd, Sydney, August, 1952.
Jaybird Genealogies. www.pitt.edu.
Encyclopedia Britannica. 1911 edition.
Iron Trade Review and Beaton Institute. Extract from Lorain Journal, July 18, 1959.
Moxham, AJ. *Canada as a Steel Producer*. In Mining and Metallurgical number of Cassier's Magazine, 1902.
Lorain Evening Herald, Industrial Edition, 1895, and letter to authors from Lorain Public Library, October 29, 1985.
The Journal, Jan, 1983. Mahony's Memos. And MTT Monthly Bulletin, 1920 by Harold Vincent.
Beaton Institute. MG12, 57.
Sydney Record, June 6 and June 8, 1901.
Personal conversation between Pam Newton and AJ Moxham's grandson, 1985.

ONE OF MANY
Halifax Herald. August 31, 1901.
Across the Tickle. Events of 1898.
Shea, Emily. Unpublished research paper, 2003.
Cadigan, Sean T. *Hope and Deception in Conception Bay*. University of Toronto Press. 1995.
Family recollections of Dennis Shea, Conception Bay South, Nfld.
Sydney Record, June 10, 1901

BLACK STEEL WORKERS FROM ALABAMA
Newton, David. *Tainted Justice, 1914*. UCCB Press. 1995.
Sydney Record. Dec 21 1901. from Chattanooga, Tennessee. "J.H. Means has left on his return to Nova Scotia with three carloads of Tennessee and Alabama Negroes who will go to work in the furnace there."
Beaton, Elizabeth. *An Afro-American Community in Cape Breton, 1901-1904*. Beaton Institute. March 23, 1995. In passim.
Bangor Daily News, January 13, 1903.

CAPTAIN HORSFALL AND THE SCHOOL FOR SCANDAL
Sydney Record – early 1903

ROBERT J. PEARY, NORTHWARD HO!
Berton, Pierre. The Arctic Grail.
Jackson, Elva E. North Sydney: Windows on the Past.

"THOSE DARING YOUNG MEN AND THEIR FLYING MACHINES"
Sydney Post, Sept 22, 1909.
His spacious home on Kings Road later became the Wandlyn Hotel
Ibid
Encyclopedia Britannica, 1911 ed.
Brown, R J. Alexander Graham Bell and the Garfield Assassination. in the History Buff.
Magnusson, Magnus. Chambers Biographical Dictionary. 1990.
Baddeck Public Library. The Search for Yesterday. The Silver Dart. April, 1981.
Wraga, William. Glenn Hammond Curtiss. Curtis Wright Corporation. History 1876-1908.
Cape Breton Post, July 22, 1960. Article by J A D McCurdy.
Phillips, Alan. Into the Twentieth Century. Canada's Illustrated Heritage. Published Jack McClelland. 1977.

JACK HOLMES – HANGMAN
Various issues of The *Cape Breton Post* & *The Highlander*
Beaton Institute Archives, Cape Breton University
Newton, David . Tainted Justice, 1914. University College of Cape Breton Press. Sydney. 1995
Engel, Howard. Lord High Executioner. Key Porter Books Ltd. Toronto. 1996

"GUS" EDWARDS - COAL MINER TO AIR MARSAL
Frank, David. J.B. McLachlan. James Lorimer and Co. Toronto. 1999.
Ibid. p 94. Quoting AS Kendall Papers . PANS.
Wise, Sydney F. Canadian Airmen and the First World War. Toronto University Press.

COLONIAL LOGS SET SAIL
Tennyson, Brian and Sarty, Roger. Guardian of the Gulf. University of Toronto Press 2000.
His Majesty's Stationary Office. Mineral Statistics, report to Secretary for Mines. 1917-1933.
Beaton Institute. Scrapbook 15C p.47. University College of Cape Breton.

BERYL MARKHAM - "STRAIGHT ON TILL MORNING"
Interview reported in British *Daily Express* Sept 7, 1936.
Tape recording, Beaton Institute.
These recollections are at odds with some of the historically recorded events, but are remembered by those interviewed by the authors

THREE WRITERS
Warner, Charles Dudley. Baddeck and That Sort of Thing. Atlantic Monthly, Feb, Mar, Apr, 1874.
Keller, Helen, The Story of My Life.
DeBrett's Peerage.
Walsh, Edmund Fall of the Russian Empire. Chap 4.
Department of Natural Resources, Baddeck office, Ian Smith.
MacNeil, Neil. The Highland Heart in Nova Scotia. Charles Scribner's Sons, New York. 1948.
New York Times. Dec 19, 1969.
This article was previously published under the title *"Three Writers From Away"* in the *Cape Bretoner Magazine* Volume 13 No.3, Summer issue July/August 2005.

OK, SIGNED TK
Annual Reports – Cape Breton Development Corporation
Local newspaper interviews.